# THE
# ONE-MINUTE
# GARDENER

# THE
# ONE-MINUTE
# GARDENER

### It Sounds Incredible—But You Really Can Have a Successful Garden with Just One Minute of Care Each Day

Text and Photography by Derek Fell

Running Press Book Publishers
Philadelphia, Pennsylvania

A FRIEDMAN GROUP BOOK

Copyright © 1988 by Michael Friedman Publishing Group, Inc.

9  8  7  6  5  4  3  2  1

Digit on the right indicates the number of this printing.

Library of Congress Cataloging-in-Publication Number:
87-42983

ISBN 0-89471-589-5 (Cloth)

*THE ONE-MINUTE GARDENER;*
*It Sounds Incredible—But You Really Can Have a Successful Garden*
*with Just One Minute of Care Each Day*
was prepared and produced by Michael Friedman Publishing Group, Inc.
15 West 26th Street
New York, New York 10010

Editor: Tim Frew
Copy Editor: Mary Forsell
Art Director: Mary Moriarty
Production Manager: Karen L. Greenberg

Typeset by Lettering Directions
Color separations by Hong Kong Scanner Craft Company Ltd.
Printed and bound in Hong Kong by Leefung-Asco Printers Ltd.

This book may be ordered from the Publisher.
Please include $1.50 postage.
**But try your bookstore first.**

Running Press Book Publishers
125 South Twenty-Second Street
Philadelphia, Pennsylvania 19103

# ABOUT THE AUTHOR

DEREK FELL HAS BEEN GARDENING FOR MORE THAN twenty-five years and currently cultivates a two-acre garden in Bucks County, Pennsylvania. A consultant on vegetable gardening to the White House during the Ford administration, he has served as executive director of All-America Selections (the national seed trials) and the National Garden Bureau (an information office sponsored by the American seed industry).

Fell devised the concept behind *The One-Minute Gardener* out of necessity during a period of his life when he had an extremely demanding schedule, but did not want to eliminate the pleasures of gardening from his agenda.

He is a director of the Garden Writers Association of America and has won numerous awards for garden photography and writing. He is a regular contributor to such publications as *Architectural Digest,* the *New York Times Magazine, Connoisseur, Americana, Woman's Day,* and *Garden Design* and is also author of numerous garden books and calendars.

E     N     T     S

# INTRODUCTION

*The author displays the typical early-summer production from a one-minute flower garden. Baskets filled with flowering annuals will be used to create floral arrangements indoors. Proper choices of annuals ensure that the garden remains colorful until fall frosts.*

IN THIS BUSY, FAST-PACED WORLD, WHERE PEOPLE BARELY have enough time to devote to their jobs and families, there just don't seem to be enough hours in the day to cultivate a gratifying garden of vegetables and flowers. Gardens are a lot of fun, and most people recognize the benefits of beauty from flowers and nutrition from fresh vegetables. However, gardens are associated with work, so most busy people either abandon the idea of a beautiful and bountiful garden altogether or else they make a well-intentioned start only to give up when weeds, drought, insects, or diseases threaten to take over. With the one-minute garden, however, that doesn't need to happen any longer. Neither a gimmick nor an exaggeration, this gardening system ensures results. Once planted, the up-to-date, easy-care gardening methods described in this book take an average of only one minute a day, or seven minutes per week, of "aftercare" for up to 500 square feet (46 square meters) of garden. Even the ordinarily tiresome tasks of weeding, watering, fertilizing, and insect and disease control require this brief expenditure of time.

This book is organized into two parts: *The One-Minute Vegetable Garden* and *The One-Minute Flower Garden*. Perhaps a nearly maintenance-free garden sounds implausible, but it is possible! The secret lies in proper planning and planting, so that once the garden is planted aftercare takes only a minute a day. Many people don't mind the work involved in preparing and planting a garden—it's the battle of the bugs, the havoc of weeds, death by drought, impoverished plants, and the curse of diseases that often prove time-consuming and frustrating. When days get hot and humid during summer, many a well-planted garden becomes too demanding of time. The secret of success with the one-minute garden is that, once planted, the garden almost takes care of itself, except for the delightful chore of harvesting, which actually takes more time than all the care needed.

Unfortunately, there have been many gardening systems that promise labor-saving results, and it's only natural for people to be skeptical of these claims. Other methods have been presented under an array of promising titles, but none of these systems can come close to the savings in time and energy that the one-minute garden delivers. This system has been tested over a period of seven years and is acclaimed by many impartial gardeners who have tried it for themselves.

What's more, the one-minute-garden concept delivers nothing less than superb results. In fact, the one-minute-garden system can grow vegetables and flowers *better* than other methods, producing ears of sweet corn that are 28 inches (70 centimeters) long, tomatoes the size of grapefruits, giant bell peppers as much as 10 inches (25 centimeters) long, and zucchini squash yielding in twenty days from planting. Using the techniques outlined in this book, you will grow vegetables that are bigger, more flavorful, and more abundant than those produced using traditional methods. Additionally, they will come to maturity earlier than you ever thought possible. Flowers, too, yield sensational results. You will be rewarded with such special touches as uniform rows of petunias, marigolds that provide long-lasting color, bloom-smothered plants, and an array of bright, bold floral colors.

All these gardening feats are made possible by combining several good practices—good soil preparation (the foundation of any successful garden), wide-row planting for efficient utilization of space, regular amounts of water through inexpensive systems of drip irrigation, automatic weed control through a simple systems of mulching, automatic feeding through new methods of fertilizing, efficient insect control through organic insect sprays that are fast and easy to apply, and some built-in hygienic elements (including the use of special disease-resistant plants) to help control the majority of plant diseases. Think of it—super soil, properly spaced plants, water at the turn of a faucet, automatic weed control, automatic feeding, safe insect control and freedom from disease—all requiring a fraction of your day. There simply isn't a more pleasurable, more efficient, or more rewarding way to garden.

# PART 1

## THE
# ONE-MINUTE
# VEGETABLE
# GARDEN

# CHAPTER 1

■

# PLANNING AND SOIL PREPARATION

■

## Drawing Up A Plan

THE FIRST STEP TOWARD A ONE-MINUTE GARDEN IS TO PLAN ON PAPER THE GARDEN size and selection of plant varieties. The most efficient layout for a one-minute vegetable garden is raised planting beds 15 feet (4½ meters) long by 2 feet (60 centimeters) wide and 4-to-8 inches (10-to-20 centimeters) high, with 12-to-24-inch (30-to-60-centimeter) walkways between planting beds. The reason for a 15-foot row length is that most seed packets are based on supplying sufficient seed to plant a 15-foot (4½-meter) row.

A wide, raised bed provides good drainage, increases soil depth so plants can grow vigorous root systems for maximum yields, and makes it more efficient to cultivate. Without a clearly defined planting area, valuable resources—soil conditioners, fertilizer, and water—can be wasted on walkways. Raised planting rows do not need to be boxed in—indeed, it is better if they are not as this hampers irrigation. The soil can be simply mounded above the surrounding walkways to create a raised row.

A seed catalog is a good place to begin your variety selections. Usually these are mailed out in January, and even if you intend to use plants purchased from a garden center instead of starting with seeds, a seed catalog will help you decide what to plant and how many days it takes grow vegetables until harvest time.

Another basic step for creating a successful one-minute vegetable garden is selecting a sunny site that drains well. Vegetables need at least six hours of sunlight each day, but the more the better. If the site has poor drainage and cannot be improved by some form of drainage system (such as pipes), consider putting down a surface of crushed stones and building up a raised area bordered with railroad ties.

*The most efficient planting system for vegetables is an area that is square or rectangular in shape, featuring wide, raised rows 15 feet (4.5 meters) long, 2 feet (60 centimeters) wide, 4 to 6 inches (10 to 15 centimeters) high, and with a 12-inch (30-centimeter) walkway between each row. Here, soil is being raked up from walkways to create a raised planting row.*

## Preparing The Soil

A SUCCESSFUL ONE-MINUTE GARDEN ALSO DEPENDS ON GOOD SOIL, WHICH NOT only serves to anchor plants firmly, but also provides them with nutrients and moisture. With new gardens especially, it is useful to use a soil test that indicates the fertility and composition of your soil. In the United States, except in the states of California and Illinois, where all soil tests are done by private laboratories, the simplest way to have your soil tested is to contact your local county agent's office. He or she will send you a pouch to fill with soil from different areas of your plot, for mailing to your state university. Back will come a computer print-out stating the pH content of your soil and its nutrient levels. The print-out will also advise how much fertilizer to apply to bring nutrient levels up to standard and also what to add to improve the pH level.

A soil's acidity or alkalinity is measured by pH. Generally, vegetables like a slightly acidic soil, but if the soil is too acidic, then limestone is added to bring the acidity down. Conversely, if the soil is too alkaline then the report may recommend that sulfur be added. An important factor that a soil test does not show is the humus content of your soil. Lack of humus (organic matter) can make it difficult for plant roots to absorb nutrients. For example, sandy soil has no holding capacity and allows nutrients to escape quickly; clay soil is too compacted, hard, and cold, making it impossible for plant roots to penetrate freely. Where soil texture is poor, soil conditioners should be added to increase the organic content.

A complete listing of state and provincial soil-testing centers begins on page 92.

## AMENDMENTS

Soil can be classified into three types: sand, clay, and loam. Sand is made up of large soil particles that drain so quickly that they won't hold mositure or nutrients. Clay is made up of fine soil particles packed together so tightly they form slimy lumps, which are prone to waterlogging. Loam soil is just right—a crumbly texture that holds moisture but lets any excess water drain away freely. Loam soils have high humus content—organic matter supplied from decomposed animal and vegetable waste, such as garden compost, leaf mold, animal manure, and peat moss. To improve both sandy and clay soils the remedy is the same—lots of organic matter.

*Planting and Installing Your One-Minute Vegetable Garden*

*1. Stake out an area 17 feet (5 meters) wide by 31 feet (9.4 meters) long, choosing a site as level as possible that is exposed to full sun and has good drainage.*

*2. Spread soil conditioner over the site. Compost taken from a home-made compost pile is particularly desirable. Alternatively, use well-decomposed, stable manure, leaf mold, spent mushroom soil, peat moss, or any other material with high humus content.*

*3. A soil test performed through your local state or provincial extension service can give you more accurate information about the nature of your soil and how to correct it for maximum vegetable production. Mix lime and fertilizer into the upper soil surface by raking. In alkaline soil areas, substitute peat moss for lime.*

*Planting and Installing Your One-Minute Vegetable Garden*

5. *Snake drip irrigation hose up and down the raised rows, making sure it rests in the middle of each row so plants or seeds can be placed on either side of it.*

4. *Mound soil into wide, parallel, raised beds 2 feet (60 centimeters) across the top by raking soil from the walkways to form raised beds of lightly pulverized soil, each 2 foot (60 centimeters) raised row separated by a 1 foot (30 centimeters) walkway.*

6. *Test drip hose after placing it in position to ensure it is free from blockage or leaks.*

7. On a calm, windless day, lay black plastic mulch over the raised rows, anchoring the edges with loose soil so the wind cannot get underneath and blow it away.

Mulch with straw between the rows and along the walkways to control weeds that can grow there. Mulching also ensures that walkways won't get muddy.

8. Create planting stations for seeds or transplants. Using a sharp pair of scissors, simply cut crosses in the plastic and peel back the corners so you can dig holes.

9. To control pests, spray plants early with a liquid pesticide. Organic gardeners can use an organic spray made from rotenone and pyrethrum. In combination, the two control a wide range of insect pests.

In areas where slugs are a menace, put down shallow dishes of slug bait marked "safe for vegetable gardens."

*Planting and Installing Your One-Minute Vegetable Garden*

10. *An initial fertilizer application at the beginning of the season may not be enough to sustain high yields for long, so supplemental applications of fertilizer are often needed. You can accomplish this either by inserting a fertilizer applicator into your drip irrigation line or by making a liquid feed and spraying it onto the leaves of plants.*

11. *Feeding, spraying for insects, weed control, and irrigation requires a brief expenditure of time. The one-minute vegetable garden almost takes care of itself.*

12. *The only part of the one-minute vegetable garden that isn't automatic is harvesting. But what a pleasure it is to go into your garden every morning and pick loads of fresh vegetables.*

Peat moss is readily available from garden centers and makes an excellent soil conditioner, but it can be expensive for treating large areas. Stable manure (well decomposed) is usually much less expensive. Also, you can start a compost pile by heaping garden and kitchen waste into a bin or mound (see page 64 for more on composting). Piles of leaves create leaf mold. It is the finest kind of humus you can add to soil since it is usually rich in trace elements, though lime may need to be added to reduce acidity.

It is impossible to add too much organic matter to garden soil. Many of the best vegetable gardens are pure organice matter, built up over the years on top of impoverished soil.

## FERTILIZERS

One-minute gardens require high soil fertility. If you add garden compost at the start of each planting season you will automatically add nutrients, but to meet the high nutrient needs of most modern vegetables (especially hybrids) it is best to add a commercial fertilizer to the soil at the beginning of the planting season. Fertilizers contain three major plant nutrients—*nitrogen* for healthy leaves, *phosphorus* for healthy roots and fruit formation, and *potash* for disease resistance. The numbers on a fertilizer bag correspond with the percentages of each nutrient. For example, 5-10-5 means 5 percent nitrogen, 10 percent phosphorus, and 5 percent potash—a total of 20 percent nutrient content, with the rest being filler.

Between digging the soil and raking it level, take a general-purpose granular fertilizer (such as 5-10-5) and spread it over the soil surface at the rate recommended on the label. Rake this into the soil thoroughly. If your soil also needs liming or an application of sulfur to alter the pH, do this at the same time so both fertilizer and soil amendment are raked in together.

Later in the season, particularly when plants start to set fruit, vegetables benefit from booster applications of fertilizer. This is best done by *foliar feeding*, using a liquid fertilizer diluted with water at the rate recommended on the label. Just fill a spray bottle with the liquid and spray it onto foliage. Plants then absorb nutrients through their leaves. Foliar spraying of fertilizer is much faster than spreading granular fertilizer around root zones.

## DIGGING THE SITE

Digging garden soil prior to planting is beneficial because it helps break up compacted soil, lets air into the soil, and allows you to remove stones, trash, and weed roots. Also, at the same time you are turning over the soil, and before it is raked over, you can be mixing in such soil amendments as lime, organic matter, and fertilizer. Generally speaking, vegetables need a crumbly soil to a depth of 12 inches (30 centimeters). Deeper digging will not hurt, but it is better to concentrate your efforts on having the top 12 inches (30 centimeters) in prime condition than to dissipate your efforts in "double digging" just to get extra soil depth. More than 90 percent of a plant's nutrient and moisture intake will occur in the first twelve inches of soil.

With one-minute vegetable gardens, it is necessary to dig the soil *only during the first year*. In subsequent years, no heavy digging with a spade or tiller is needed, because the soil has been mounded into convenient 2 foot (60-centimeter) wide raised rows that stay crumbly from year to year. Just run a long-handled cultivator along the top of the raised row to break the crust that usually forms during winter and mix in fresh supplies of humus, fertilizer, and lime, if needed. The soil amendments can be broadly cast over the surface and quickly worked into the soil with a rake to get each row ready for a new planting season.

Digging the first year can be done by renting a power tiller or by using a shovel. It is important to break up any thick clumps with the edge of your spade and remove from the soil any grubs, stones, and weed roots you unearth.

## Tips on One-Minute Soil Preparation

- A small, well-tended area will yield far more than a large area that is neglected.

- Limit your garden to less than 500 square feet (46 square meters) during the first year.

- Try to locate your vegetable plot near the house. This makes it easy to slip out before mealtimes to gather fresh produce, and it keeps your garden within reach of a water faucet.

- Do-it-yourself pH soil test kits are not as economical or as accurate as having a soil laboratory test your soil.

- Earthworms improve soil by ingesting soil particles and expelling them as castings that are richer in nutrients than the soil they ingest. Usually you do not need to buy earthworms. Their eggs are present in all cultivated soils. Just add lots of organic material to increase their populations.

- Leaf mold is the very finest soil conditioner to add to garden soil. To create leaf mold, collect fallen leaves, shred them with a lawn mower and pile them into a bin made from chicken wire. Left to decompose for a year, the resulting leaf mold can be applied to garden soil as a mulch.

# C H A P T E R  2

# LAYOUT AND
# PLANTING

ALTHOUGH PLANTING PLANS CAN BE VARIED TO SUIT DIFFERENT GARDEN SPACES, the most popular and most efficient layout for a one-minute vegetable garden is a rectangular plot facing west. This way, as the sun travels across the sky from east to west taller plants in the garden do not shade shorter plants. Positioning taller plants at the north end of the garden also avoids shading.

## Making Raised Beds

THE MOST EFFICIENT PLANTING PLAN IS A RECTANGULAR PLOT, SIZE 17 FEET (5 meters) wide by 31 feet (9½ meters) long. A total of ten raised rows are made 2 feet (60 centimeters) wide 4 to 8 inches (10 to 20 centimeters) high, with a walkway between each row. The walkway should be at least 12 inches (30 centimeters) wide. The raised rows are made by raking soil between the walkways into mounds and leveling the top with a rake. The raised rows can also be made by adding loads of compost or by hauling in good garden topsoil from another location if the present soil is poor. Each raised row runs to 15 feet (4½ meters) in length, plus 12 inches (30 centimeters) of working space at each end. After the raised beds have been mounded, and before the top is raked level, soil amendments and fertilizer can be added simultaneously—fertilizer, peat moss, and lime, for example. What a good feeling it is to know that every grain of fertilizer, every shred of peat moss and every particle of lime is being used to good effect—exactly where plant roots will grow, and not a bit wasted on walkways.

The 2-foot (60-centimeter) planting width is important since it is a uniform measurement that allows plants to occupy the space efficiently. For example, small plants such as spinach, lettuce, and beans can be planted in double rows, while large plants, such as tomatoes, peppers, and corn, can be planted in a single line. Some vegetables, like onions, can be planted four abreast along the wide row.

Since the width of the rows and the width of the walkways is critical in making every bit of space count, the best way to ensure the right spacing is by using string as a guide. First use string to outline the rectangle. Turn over all the soil within the

*An efficient way to stake tomatoes is with a cylinder made from builder's wire. As the plant grows tall, it pushes side branches through the gaps and becomes self-supporting, with no training or tying needed.*

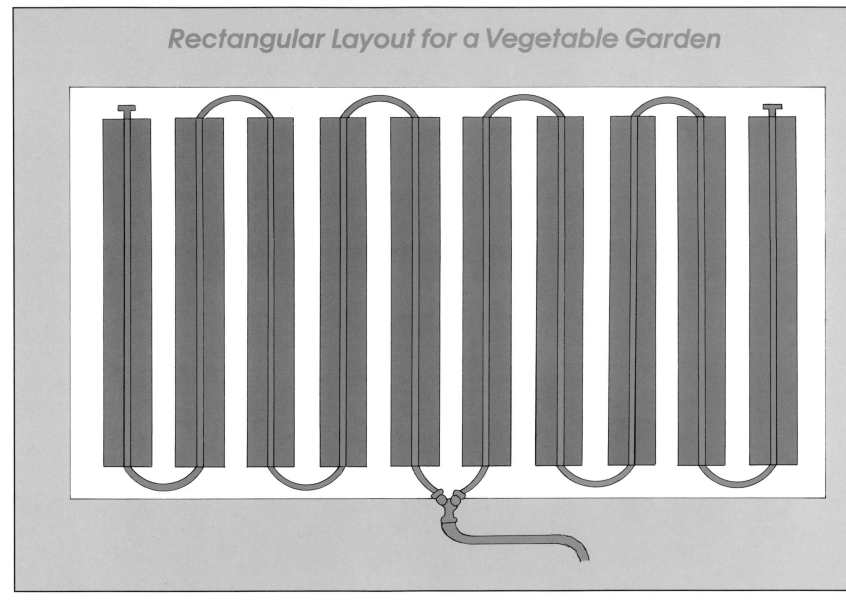

Rectangular Layout for a Vegetable Garden

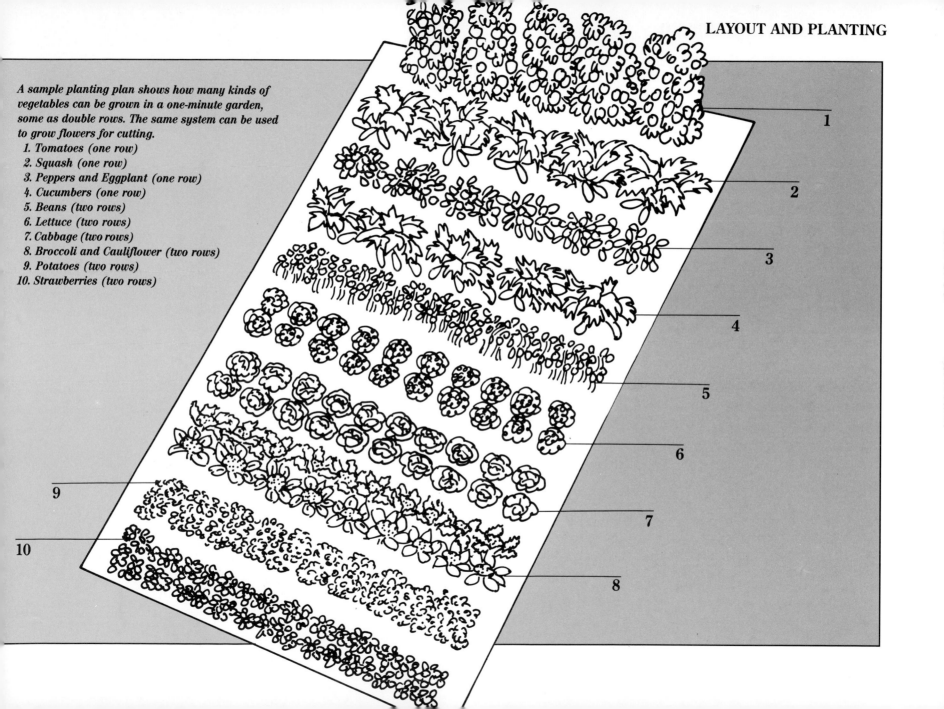

*A sample planting plan shows how many kinds of vegetables can be grown in a one-minute garden, some as double rows. The same system can be used to grow flowers for cutting.*

1. *Tomatoes (one row)*
2. *Squash (one row)*
3. *Peppers and Eggplant (one row)*
4. *Cucumbers (one row)*
5. *Beans (two rows)*
6. *Lettuce (two rows)*
7. *Cabbage (two rows)*
8. *Broccoli and Cauliflower (two rows)*
9. *Potatoes (two rows)*
10. *Strawberries (two rows)*

outlined area. Then measure off the walkways and row widths with a yardstick or tape measure, placing sticks to show the position of rows. Then, using string to ensure accuracy, create each raised row one at a time ensuring it is 2 feet (60 centimeters) wide by 4 to 8 inches (10 to 20 centimeters) high. Remember, you can do this using soil from the walkways.

Once you have raised rows and walkways defined you will discover that no further digging of the garden is needed from year to year. All you have to do is disturb the surface of each raised row with a hand cultivator, mixing in fertilizer and soil amendments to replenish the soil. So, the extra care it takes to prepare your site the first year is a one-time investment. Once the raised bed system is in place it stays that way forever, no further digging or raking necessary.

## Irrigation

THROUGHOUT MOST OF NORTH AMERICA, SUMMERS TEND TO BE HOT AND DRY. Therefore, it is risky for the gardener to plant a vegetable garden and then rely on natural rainfall to keep it healthy. It is unnecessary to take such a gamble when economical and efficient methods of irrigation are available to water whole sections of gardens at the mere turn of a water faucet. The installation of a drip irrigation system in particular is a sound investment and probably the very best investment a gardener could make for ensuring success.

Adequate watering is an essential in the one-minute vegetable garden system. Moisture *in regular amounts* is important to plant growth. Plants can only take in nutrients from the soil in *soluble form*, diluted with water. Even the sugars responsible for flavor in vegetables move into the edible parts in liquid form. Without moisture, plants can quickly come under water stress, slow down or stop growing altogether, and finally wilt; radishes become pithy in flavor; cantaloupes taste bland; sweet corn fails to fill out at the tips and develops distorted ears; tomatoes develop blossom-end rot; cucumbers prematurely stop growing; watermelons develop hollow

insides; lettuce and other leaf crops taste bitter. Even three days without rainfall can put many vegetables under stress (beets, turnips, and radishes are notable examples). Tests conducted on commercial vegetable crops have proven that where drainage is good, plants benefit from being watered *every day*. That way, they grow fast, take in adequate nutrients, develop full size and flavor, and produce highest yields and attractive color.

In the world of vegetable gardening there are three ways to water a garden when natural rainfall is lacking. Some people stand around with garden hoses and water plants by hand; others even use a watering can. This method is not only time-consuming, but it is also inefficient because it always seems as if you are putting more water into the soil than you really are. Another inefficient method is to let a lawn sprinkler drench the garden overnight while you sleep. This is wasteful since you are watering areas that don't need water (like walkways). Also, tests have proven that frequent overhead watering like this promotes fungus diseases like mildew. Also, lawn sprinklers often need moving around to cover an area completely, and they waste a lot of water from evaporation. A third method, and by far the most favorable one, is to employ a drip irrigation system that uses hoses lying on top of the soil to soak the root zone. Water travels through the entire length of the hose at the turn of a faucet. No water touches the leaves or is wasted on walkways. The flow is regulated so that a person can leave for three weeks on vacation and have the hose line drip minuscule amounts of water the entire period, keeping the plot sufficiently moist to prevent moisture stress without waterlogging the soil. By covering the drip system with mulch—particularly straw or black plastic—there is no moisture loss through evaporation. Every precious drop goes to benefit your plants.

Nor do you need a water faucet to work some drip systems. At least two brands are so efficient at irrigating that they will work from gravity pressure, hooked up to a rain barrel or water tank raised off the ground.

*Left: The author stands in the middle of a one-minute vegetable garden in early spring with a harvest of fresh greens. The layout for this garden matches the design on page 25.*

## INSTALLING DRIP IRRIGATION

For years the technical world has been searching for a system of drip irrigation that saturates the soil yet does not clog with soil particles or algae after extended use. There are two kinds of drip irrigation systems that try to avoid this: the *soaker hose* type, whereby tiny pores in the hose wall "sweat" droplets of moisture along the entire hose length; and the *emitter* type, whereby drip stations are spaced at equal distances. In my experience, the soaker system works best.

First, the cost is reasonable. For about twenty-five dollars (thirty-two Canadian dollars, fifteen pounds) it's possible to irrigate 500 square feet (46 square meters) of garden, and the hose is reusable if it is taken up in the autumn and stored under cover.

Also, soaker systems are the only kind that can work with low water pressure and can be connected to a reservoir or rain barrel raised above the ground for gravity feeding.

To install a drip irrigation hose in a one-minute vegetable garden, just unroll the hose along the middle of each row, snaking the hose from one raised bed to the next, up and down the rows. Stakes at the end of each row will help to loop the hose around the ends so it doesn't pull out of alignment and stays perfectly centered. Having the hose centered allows planting on both sides of it. The most efficient layout is one whereby two sections of drip hose are connected to a water source by means of a "Y" valve. Each side of the "Y" has a shutoff valve so that one-half of the garden can be irrigated without the other, in the event that one-half the garden is planted early and the other late.

After the hose is laid down it is vital to test the flow to ensure there are no obstructions such as a twist in the line. Once the line has been tested and water has filled the hose completely from end to end, it is important to cover the hose, either with an organic mulch such as straw or by using black plastic. This protects the hose from damage by stray animals and from the destructive ultraviolet rays of the sun.

*Above: This holding tank for a gravity-feed system to irrigate a vegetable or flower garden can be made from a plastic or metal trash container. The tank is raised above soil level, and the drip irrigation system transmits the water to planting rows.*

## DRIP IRRIGATION SYSTEMS

Following is a description of the most widely sold drip irrigation systems. For sources see page 92.

*Burpee Dripline Kit.* Drip stations are pre-spaced along flexible tubing at 2 foot (60 centimeters) intervals. This kit consists of 25 feet (7.5 meters) of leader hose plus fourteen 15 foot (4.6 meters) drip lines leading off in parallel rows to irrigate 375 square feet (35 square meters). Cost is about thirty-five dollars (forty-six Canadian dollars, twenty-one pounds). Larger and smaller kits are available.

*Irrigro.* Porous plastic tubing trickles water through pores along the hose. Works with low water pressure for connecting to well systems, mains, or resevoirs. Doesn't easily clog. This is the most inexpensive system to install—leader hose plus 100 feet (30 meters) of tubing (sufficient for 250 square feet [23 square meters] of garden space), cost about fifteen dollars (twenty Canadian dollars, nine pounds). A kit to cover 500 square feet (46 square meters) costs about twenty-five dollars (thirty-two Canadian dollars, fifteen pounds).

*Leaky Pipe.* Also sold under the name "Root Quencher." Rubber tubing made from recycled tires leaks moisture along its length. Works with low water pressure. Extremely durable. Leader hose plus 100 feet (30 meters) of tubing to cover 250 square feet, (23 square meters) costs about sixty-five dollars (eighty-five Canadian dollars, forty pounds).

*Submatic Drip Irrigation.* Drippers are pre-spaced along poly-flex tubing at 2 foot (60 centimeters) intervals. Kit consisting of 200 feet (60 meters) of hose to cover 500 square feet (46 square meters) of garden space, costs about forty-seven dollars (sixty-one Canadian dollars, twenty-nine pounds).

*Below: Diagram shows how a Y valve connects to a water faucet or tank by means of a garden hose, and how two sets of feeder tubing lead off to connect with a drip irrigation system.*

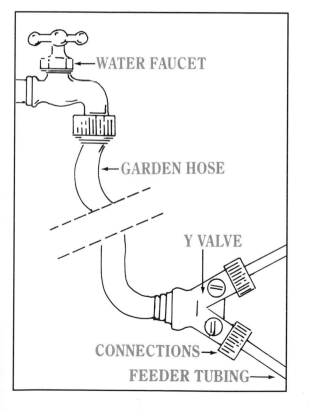

WATER FAUCET

GARDEN HOSE

Y VALVE

CONNECTIONS→

FEEDER TUBING→

*Left: Straw not only acts as a mulch to control weeds, but also contributes an attractive appearance in this one-minute garden. Gardens can be mulched entirely with straw, straw on top of plastic, or fiber mulches for cosmetic effect. Below: This garden is mulched with a combination of black plastic for the planting rows and straw for the walkways. Putting straw in the walkways prevents feet from getting muddy after irrigation or rain. Black plastic raises soil temperature to benefit warm-weather crops like the zucchini squash pictured here.*

## *Mulching*

*MULCHING* IS ESSENTIAL IN A ONE-MINUTE VEGETABLE GARDEN. IT NOT ONLY protects the drip hose from damage and holds it in place once it is laid down, but it also acts as a barrier against weeds and helps conserve moisture in the soil. For weed control, different mulches have different degrees of efficiency. Organic mulches—such as straw, pine needles, and grass clippings—generally need replenishing throughout the season or stubborn weeds will still manage to get through where wind or natural decomposition creates bare spots. By far the most efficient and least expensive mulch system is *black plastic*. If you are concerned about its cosmetic appearance in the garden, use a brown plastic or brown fiber mulch or cover the black plastic with a light layer of organic mulch. An important point to remember about mulches is that organic mulches—particularly straw, pine needles, and grass clippings—will tend to cool the soil and slow down growth of warm weather crops such as tomatoes and melons. Black plastic, on the other hand, warms up the soil and has other advantages explained below.

A little less than 150 feet (45 meters) of black plastic 3 feet (1 meter) wide is needed to cover the drip irrigation hose and raised beds in a one-minute vegetable garden occupying 500 square feet (46 square meters). It is readily available from garden centers in springtime in 1 or 1½ mil thickness, and it is inexpensive.

Black plastic provides the following benefits, compared to other kinds of mulches:

- Better protection for the drip irrigation hose than organic mulches.

- A more effective barrier against weeds than organic mulches.

- It conserves moisture in the soil and reduces moisture loss through evaporation more effectively than organic mulches.

- It warms the soil early and provides stable soil temperature for rapid early growth and continuous productivity.

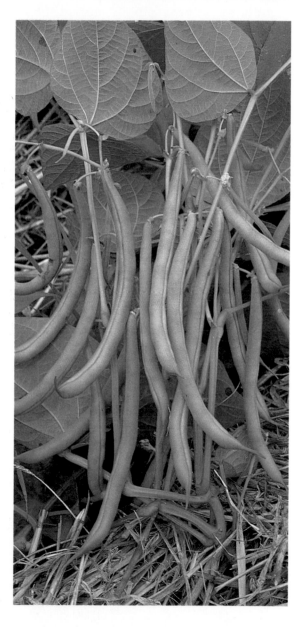

- It keeps fruit clean, preventing fruit from touching bare soil and contracting rot diseases or blemishes from mud.

- It forms a barrier against many troublesome soil pests. When maggot flies find no easy entry into the soil, for example, they look elsewhere to lay their eggs.

Even in warm climates the use of black plastic as a mulch is recommended. Plant growth soon shades the plastic during the heat of summer to prevent its overheating the soil. If extra protection is needed in warm climates, spread grass clippings (or other organic material) on top as a cooling layer to break the force of the sun's heat. Alternatively, use a biodegradable fiber mulch, also called a horticultural blanket.

Laying black plastic for a one-minute vegetable garden is easy, though it is best to choose a calm day since wind can blow the plastic about. Just take a 50- or 100-foot (15- or 30-meter) roll, anchor one end with a heavy stone at the start of a raised row and unroll the plastic to the end of the row. Using a pair of scissors, cut the plastic off where it ends the row, weight the end down with another stone, and spread the edges of the plastic so they drape snugly over the raised row. The edges of the plastic can be weighted down with soil.

Planting through black plastic is easy. With a yardstick in one hand and a pair of scissors in the other, simply cut planting stations in the form of a cross at the required distances. Spacing for each planting depends on the type of vegetable to be planted (see cultural advice for each vegetable starting on page 44).

Seeds can be sown into each planting station, or ready-grown transplants can be used. With seeds, just scoop out a depression, sprinkle a group of seeds into it and cover with soil. When the seed has sprouted thin out all but the strongest-looking plants.

Using transplants saves a lot of time. Just take a hand trowel, scoop a hole to accommodate the root ball and firm the soil back around the plant. This gives you a head start on the planting season. You can either grow your own transplants from seed or buy them ready-grown from a garden center. For more information on seed starting and buying quality transplants, see page 38. The cultural information starting on page 44 tells you how long it takes to grow your own transplants from seed.

## Mulch Blankets

*Left and below: Harvests from a one-minute garden all grown by the author.*

IN ADDITION TO BLACK PLASTIC, THERE ARE CHOICE COMMERCIAL MULCH SUB-stitutes, mostly offering the advantage of moisture penetration so that natural rainfall or sprinkler systems can irrigate the garden in the absence of drip irrigation. There are three popular varieties.

*Agripaper Natural Mulch* is a heavy paper mulch with good water penetration. The paper is tan colored on one side to blend in with soil and is biodegradable. The other side is colored black for use with crops that like warm soil temperatures, such as tomatoes and melons. It is available in rolls that are 2 feet (60 centimeters) wide by 50 feet (15 meters) long.

*du Pont Landscape Fabric* is a fiber blanket that rolls out like black plastic, but has the advantage of permitting good moisture penetration. It is charcoal gray in color and comes in rolls that are 3 feet (1 meter) wide by 50 feet (15 meters) long.

*Miracle Plastic Mulch* is similar to black plastic, but colored brown to blend in with soil. Additionally, it contains microscopic holes to permit better moisture penetration than black plastic alone. It comes in rolls that are 3 feet (1 meter) wide by 100 feet (30 meters) long.

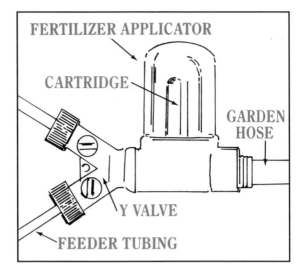

FERTILIZER APPLICATOR

CARTRIDGE

GARDEN HOSE

Y VALVE

FEEDER TUBING

*An automatic fertilizer applicator fits between a garden hose and Y valve to automatically feed plants.*

## Fertilizing

IF A GRANULAR FERTILIZER IS MIXED INTO THE SOIL PRIOR TO LAYING THE DRIP irrigation and mulch, transplants will have enough nutrients to get them off to a good start. However, when plants start to flower and develop fruit they often need booster applications of fertilizer. The easiest way to do this is by *foliar feeding*. In addition to taking up nutrients through their roots, plants are efficient at absorbing nutrients through their leaves. Since it's much easier to spray the foliage of plants with a liquid feed than to try to apply granular fertilizer by hand around the base of each plant, foliar feeding as a booster application is recommended for the one-minute vegetable garden. For the best effect, the foliar feed should be in a 1-2-1 ratio of plant nutrients, such as 5-10-5, 10-20-10 or 7-14-7. Just mix the fertilizer with a gallon of water at the rate recommended on the label, pour it into a pump-action sprayer and spray it over and under the leaves. It takes less than five minutes to do ten 15-foot (4½-meter) rows of plants, and the process can be repeated every two or three weeks.

An even faster way to feed the one-minute-vegetable garden is through the use of an *automatic fertilizer applicator*. This fits between a garden hose and the drip system. Fertilizer pellets are inserted into a clear plastic dome and dissolve when water flows along the hose, feeding plants as they are irrigated. It takes less than a minute to fill the applicator with fertilizer pellets, once every two weeks! Fertilizer pellets are available in two formulas—high nitrogen and high phosphorus. For leafy vegetables, use the high nitrogen fertilizer; for fruitful vegetables (tomatoes, for example), use the high phosphorus. Where both kinds need fertilizing together, use high phosphorus or place one of each into the applicator, since it easily holds two pellets.

# Timetable for Care of the One-Minute Garden

Once a one-minute garden is planted, the following schedule will take care of everything needed until harvest for a 500-square-foot (46-square-meter) garden plot.

| ACTIVITY | TIME | AVERAGE PER WEEK |
|---|---|---|
| *Feeding* (using automatic fertilizer applicator) | 2 minutes every 14 days | 1 minute |
| *Irrigation* (using drip system) | 1 minute every 7 days | 1 minute |
| *Weeding* (using black plastic mulch) | 0 minutes | 0 minutes |
| *Pest Control* (using organic spray) | 10 minutes every 14 days | 5 minutes |
| *Disease Control* (using disease-resistant plants) | 0 minutes | 0 minutes |
| Total Time: | | 7 minutes per week |

## *Pest and Disease Control*

IN ORDER TO CONTROL INSECT PESTS IN A ONE-MINUTE VEGETABLE GARDEN, IT IS essential to use a pesticide spray that controls the majority of insect pests. Spraying plants is by far the easiest way to attack insect pests, but many pesticides are chemical compounds that can leave harmful residues in the soil. For the one-minute vegetable garden, an organic pesticide is recommended—in particular, a formulation that combines both *rotenone* (a powder made from the roots of a tropical tree) and *pyrethrum* (a powder made from the petals of an African daisy). It's important to have the double impact of both these organic pesticides because each tends to control a different group of insects. Together, they present a broad-spectrum control. For greatest efficiency it is best to use the pyrethrum-rotenone combination in liquid form, mixing a liquid concentrate with a gallon of water at the rate recommended on the label for spraying onto foliage. To be effective, the pyrethrum-rotenone spray must be applied weekly. When it is washed off leaf surfaces by rainfall it does not leave harmful residues in the soil, but simply disintegrates and decomposes into harmless compost.

Another effective form of "safe" pest control is an insecticidal soap. Sold as a liquid concentrate, it is mixed with water for spraying on plants to control a wide range of insect pests.

The use of a drip irrigation system in a one-minute vegetable garden automatically reduces the risk of losing plants from disease, since many diseases are introduced by means of water saturating leaf surfaces. Also, the use of black plastic as a soil cover helps prevent soil diseases.

Another way to control diseases without any investment of time is to plant special disease-resistant varieties of vegetables. The cultural information starting on page 44 gives variety recommendations for major vegetable classes with built-in disease resistance. For example, if you have a soil where nematodes are a problem, then the choice of *Supersteak* hybrid tomato is recommended. It has triple disease resistance, including resistance to two common wilt diseases and nematodes. Among cucum-

*Left: These Supersteak hybrid tomatoes not only grow big and flavorful in a one-minute vegetable garden, they also have built-in pest and disease resistance. Proper selection of disease-resistant vegetables is a fundamental aspect of labor-saving garden practices. Above: Spraying with an organic liquid insecticide to control insect pests.*

# Seed-Starting Tips

*Below top: Seed trays used for starting small seeds. When seedlings are large enough to handle, they should be transferred to individual pots to make healthy transplants. Below bottom: Example of peat pots that can be used to finish off transplants.*

*The Jiffy-7 peat pot is a one-step seed starting system. Seeds germinate in the peat pot, which is held together by netting. The netting is removed at transplant time to give roots freedom to grow.*

*Large seeds like peas, beans, corn, and melons do not need pots. They can be germinated in moist paper towels and transplanted "bare root" into the garden.*

bers, disease can take a heavy toll. Plant an old-fashioned variety like *Straight Eight*, and virus diseases are likely to kill the vines before a decent crop can be harvested. But plant a variety like *Marketmore*, with many kinds of disease resistance, and it's likely you will have healthy green vines that produce continuously all season.

## *Seed Starting*

VEGETABLES CAN BE DIVIDED INTO TWO DISTINCT GROUPS: *COOL-SEASON CROPS*, which like to mature during cool conditions prevalent in spring and autumn and *warm-season crops*, which like to mature during the warm, sunny weather prevalent in summer. Cool-season vegetables include lettuce, radish, cabbage, broccoli, and spinach. Tomatoes, peppers, melons, and eggplant are some warm season vegetables. Generally speaking, cool-season vegetables will tolerate mild frosts and can be planted in the garden several weeks before the last frost date in your area. Warm-season vegetables normally are damaged by frost, so outdoor plantings should be delayed until after the last expected frost date in your area. Because of this distinction it is best to plan a one-minute vegetable garden so it is planted in two parts—one part with cool-season vegetables, the other with warm-season vegetables.

One-minute gardeners can use either seeds or plants to start their gardens. Although starting your own plants from seeds is time-consuming, and using ready-grown transplants from a garden center is labor saving, you may want to start some plants from seeds. Garden centers do not always offer a wide choice, and so you may prefer the freedom of choice that seed starting offers. There are three easy ways to start your own seeds: the *one-step* method, the *two-step* method, and *direct seeding*.

### ONE-STEP SEED STARTING
This system requires the use of either a Jiffy-7 or Jiffy-9 peat pellet. You submerge the pellet in water until it swells up to several times its original size and then plant seeds in the center of the depression located on top of the pellet. The difference

*Newly sprouted seedlings growing in a seed tray. These are now large enough to transfer into individual pots, such as the peat pots shown at the bottom left, to make sturdy transplants like those sold in garden centers.*

between Jiffy-7 and Jiffy-9 is mostly a matter of binding. The Jiffy-7 holds its peat together with a netting which is best torn away before planting to prevent the plant from becoming root-bound; the Jiffy-9 holds its peat together with an invisible binder and can be planted "as is" with no root disturbance.

After the seeds sprout, thin all but the strongest to continue growing to transplant size. At transplant time the peat pot and the plant are placed in the soil.

### TWO-STEP SEED STARTING

First, the seeds are started in trays filled with potting soil. After they have become large enough to handle, the seedlings are transferred to a peat or plastic pot filled with potting soil. When the plants reach transplant size they are transferred to the garden. With plastic pots the root ball has to be slipped out of the pot. With a peat pot it is necessary only to tear the bottom of the pot away to release the roots.

### DIRECT SEEDING

Some vegetables have large, easy-to-handle seeds that can be sown directly into the garden without the need for starting indoors. These include peas, beans, and corn. Another group of vegetables requires close spacing to be space efficient, and these also can be seeded directly into the garden. These include radishes, carrots, beets, and turnips. With the large-seeded vegetables it is still efficient to plant them through black plastic by simply sowing several seeds at each planting station and thinning the group to one plant after they are up. To save thinning, you can pregerminate large seeds in a jar of lukewarm water or in a moist paper towel. The viable seeds will swell and split their seed coats, even pushing out the beginnings of a root. Plant these viable seeds one to a planting station.

Small seeds of vegetables that take close spacing are best sown along a wide, raised row with no black plastic in place. Cast the seed along furrows, four lines abreast, and when the plants are large enough, thin them as needed. For a true one-minute vegetable garden where the objective is to keep aftercare to a minute a day, eliminate vegetables that need thinning and cannot be grown through black plastic.

# Harvests from a One-Minute Garden

These handsome golden acorn squash, called Jersey Golden, are growing on a bush plant, watered by a drip irrigation system and mulched with pine needles.

Cabbage OS Cross hybrid grows cabbage heads up to 22 pounds (10 kilograms) each. Constant moisture and protection from cabbage worms (using Dipel organic insecticide) is the key to growing impressive cabbages like these.

Above top: A total of seventy-six tomatoes were counted on this one vine—An Italian pear-type tomato—grown in just seventy days after putting transplants into a one-minute vegetable garden.
Above bottom: The Giant Walla Walla onion variety far outweighs a regular Sweet Spanish onion. Early transplanting, regular amounts of moisture, and high organic content in soil are the keys to achieving top size.

*The Supersteak hybrid, a giant-fruited tomato, easily produces tomatoes over two pounds (.9 kilograms) each in a one-minute vegetable garden. Planting through black plastic and supplying regular amounts of moisture through drip irrigation are key factors to growing flavorful, giant tomatoes.*

# C H A P T E R 3

# VEGETABLE
# SELECTIONS

Following are classes of vegetables that do well in a one-minute vegetable garden. Consider these first above all others when planning what to plant. They have been singled out either because they are easy to grow or because they give extraordinary productivity for the amount of space they occupy.

Cool-season vegetables tolerate light frosts and can be planted several weeks before the last expected frost date in spring. They prefer cool temperatures in which to mature. They can also be grown as a fall crop. Warm Season varieties are damaged by frost and must be planted after the last expected frost date. They require warm temperatures in which to mature.

*The author's son, Derek Jr., harvests tomatoes grown against a tool shed, with French marigolds planted at the base to deter nermatodes.*

## BEANS, SNAP
### Warm Season

*The bush types of snap beans take up relatively little room in comparison to yields, and these are recommended over the pole varieties. Also, they mature earlier by as much as two weeks. There are green-podded and yellow-podded kinds to choose from, and both are best grown from seeds sown directly into the garden. Plant the seeds 1 inch (2½ centimeters) deep, three or four seeds to each planting station, at the time of your last expected frost date. Space the plants six inches (15 centimeters) apart in double lines along the raised rows. Some people insist on calling snap beans "string" beans, but this name is obsolete since breeders bred the strings out of snap beans more than fifty years ago.* **Recommended varieties:** *Blue Lake, Greensleaves, Gold-crop.* **One-minute planting tip:** *Soak the seeds for one hour in lukewarm water. Plant only those beans that swell up and show viability. While the seeds are still wet, gently shake them in a bag of "inoculant"—a fine black powder that contains soil bacteria beneficial to peas and beans, resulting in substantial yield increases.*

## BEANS, LIMA
### Warm Season

*The bush types are preferred over the pole limas since they mature much earlier (by two weeks) and don't need poles for support. Lima beans do not have edible pods and must be shelled. They require almost twice the growing time of snap beans and are more sensitive to cold. Sow seeds a week or two after your last expected frost date to avoid seeds rotting in cold soil. Sow several seeds into each planting station, spacing plants at least six inches (15 centimeters) apart in double lines along raised rows.* **Recommended variety:** *Fordhook 242 (more disease resistant than regular Fordhook).* **One-minute planting tip:** *Soak the seeds in lukewarm water for one hour. Plant only those seeds that swell up and show viability.*

## BEANS, EDIBLE SOY
### Warm Season

*These compact, bushy plants offer an unusual quality among vegetables—they are rich in* protein. *Edible soy beans do not have the oily flavor of agricultural soybeans. They are sweet and tender when cooked in boiling water for just five to ten minutes. The tough, inedible pods are produced in enormous quantity, yielding two to four tender, plump, pea-size beans per pod. The pods are difficult to shell freshly picked, but they open up easily after cooking in boiling water. A favorite way to enjoy edible soybeans is as "hot snacks." After cooking just pick up a pod full of beans and press one end to squirt the beans into your mouth. They are delicious!* **Recommended variety:** *Butterbean.* **One-minute planting tip:** *Soak the seeds in lukewarm water for one hour. Plant only those seeds that swell up and show viability.*

## BEETS
### Cool Season

Beets come in several colors—regular "red" beets, yellow beets, and white beets. The seeds are grouped together in clusters and so thinning can be a tedious business. One-minute gardeners prefer to transplant beets into planting stations spaced four inches apart, four lines to a row. Garden centers regularly sell beet transplants. It can be tedious cutting plastic to make planting stations for beets, so you may prefer to use a regular organic mulch such as straw. Beets are hardy and can be planted into the garden several weeks before the last frost date. If you sow seeds, cover them with ¼ inch (½ centimeter) of soil. In order to grow tender, sweet, and succulent, beets need steady amounts of moisture. You can begin harvesting when they are the size of golf balls (baby beets). Beet tops are also good to eat. **Recommended varieties:** Golden Beet (tops taste like spinach); Pacemaker II (a hybrid with solid red cores and no fibrous rings). **One-minute planting tip**: Beets are time-consuming to grow from seed, so you may prefer to use transplants.

## BROCCOLI AND CAULIFLOWER
### Cool Season

Both these members of the cabbage family should be planted so they mature during cool weather—either in late spring or fall. The seeds need covering with ¼ inch (½ centimeter) of soil. Seeds take eight weeks to grow large enough to transplant. Once transplanted into the garden they make rapid growth, maturing within fifty to sixty days if given regular amounts of moisture. Since broccoli and cauliflower are hardy, they can be planted into the garden several weeks before the last expected frost date in spring. Proper spacing is essential for them to develop their large, solid, edible heads made up of tight bud clusters. Space the plants 18 inches (45 centimeters) apart in double lines along raised rows. Most broccoli heads are green, while cauliflower heads are white. Broccoli is the easiest to grow of the two. To keep a cauliflower head white it may be necessary to tie the jacket leaves up over the plant.

Another advantage of broccoli is its extra productivity. After the large terminal bud is harvested, smaller heads are often produced on side shoots. **Recommended varieties:** Premium Crop hybrid (best large-headed broccoli); Stove-pipe cauliflower (a self-blanching type that forms compact heads inside a funnel of long jacket leaves). **One-minute planting tip:** Buy ready-grown transplants.

## BRUSSELS SPROUTS
### Cool Season

Though not fast vegetables to grow, Brussels sprouts extend the productivity of the garden into winter months. They are so hardy that the tight bud clusters, known as sprouts, will stay firm and edible up to Christmas over most areas of the United States. They are good to plant as a "succession crop" to follow a planting of spring peas. The peas can be harvested by the end of spring and the spent vines removed; then transplants of brussels sprouts can be set into the same row. They will take about one-hundred days to mature from transplanting. Set plants at least 18 inches (45 centimeters) apart in double lines along raised rows. Cover seed with ¼ inch (½ centimeter) of soil when starting your own plants indoors. **Recommended variety:** Jade Cross hybrid for its tremendous yields (twice standard varieties). **One-minute planting tip**: Seeds take eight weeks to grow large enough to transplant. Buy ready-grown transplants.

## CABBAGE
### Cool Season

*When choosing cabbage always check the catalog or seed packet description to determine how many days to maturity. Some need only sixty days to form heads; others need more than one-hundred from the time they're transplanted. Seed takes eight weeks to make a transplant. You can choose green cabbage, savoy cabbage, red cabbage, or Chinese cabbage. Cabbages of all types are hardy and may be set into the garden several weeks before the last expected frost date. To start your own transplants plant seed ¼ inch (½ centimeter) deep. Space plants 18 inches (45 centimeters) apart in double lines along raised rows. To get the largest heads, regular amounts of moisture are needed at all stages of growth.* **Recommended varieties:** *Stonehead hybrid (disease resistant); OS Cross hybrid (mammoth-sized heads up to twenty-two pounds, or eight kilograms, each).* **One-minute planting tip:** *Buy ready-grown transplants.*

## CANTALOUPE
### Warm Season

*The secret of good cantaloupes is plenty of sunlight, warm temperatures, high soil fertility, and regular amounts of moisture. They love to be grown with their roots covered with black plastic because of their preference for warm soil. Although the seeds are easy to handle and can be sown directly into the garden, covered with ½ inch (1 centimeter) of soil, earlier yields are assured if transplants are set into the garden after all danger of frost is past. Seed takes four weeks to make a transplant. Start spraying with pesticide immediately to discourage cucumber beetles from attacking the leaves and introducing disease. "Bush" varieties of cantaloupe occupy much less space than vine types. Bush varieties can be spaced 2 feet (60 centimeters) apart in double lines along raised rows. For vine types, space them 3 feet (90 centimeters) apart in a single line. Other good melons to grow in addition to cantaloupes are honeydews and crenshaws.* **Recommended varieties:** *Sugarbush and Sweet 'n Early, both bush types.* **One-minute planting tip:** *Buy ready-grown transplants.*

## CARROTS
### Cool Season

*There is a tremendous variation in carrot shapes. Some are short and stubby for growth in shallow soils; others are long and tapering for growth in deep, loose soils. Since carrots tolerate crowding and can be planted close together, it is too tedious to grow them through black plastic. Better to sow the seed thinly on top of bare soil, cover it lightly and then deep water the soil so germination of the tiny seeds occurs fast, and their delicate tap roots penetrate the soil quickly. If you want a true one-minute vegetable garden with only a minute of aftercare per day, leave out carrots since a lot of time is needed in the early stages of development to thin them. They resent transplanting and must be started from seed sown into the planting row. Carrots are hardy, and seed can be sown several weeks before the last expected frost date.* **Recommended variety:** *Short 'n Sweet (short rooted).* **One-minute planting tip:** *Pregerminate seeds indoors in a moist paper towel.*

47

## CELERY
### Cool Season

*A fertile soil and regular amounts of moisture are needed to produce good celery. Although these plants are hardy, too many frosty nights will cause them to bolt to seed and produce poor stalks, so delay planting them in the garden until after the last frost date. If planting from seed, cover seeds with ¼ inch (½ centimeter) of fine soil. Seeds will take eight to ten weeks to produce transplants. Celery transplants easily and should be spaced 12 inches (30 centimeters) apart in double lines along raised rows. To whiten or blanch the stems so they taste extra crisp and tender, leaves or compost can be heaped up around the stalks starting several weeks before harvest. However, this is labor-intensive, and it is better to choose a "self-blanching" variety. About one-hundred days are needed to reach maturity after transplanting.* **Recommended variety:** *Fordhook Self-Blanching.* **One-minute planting tip:** *Buy ready-grown transplants.*

## CHARD, SWISS
### Cool Season

*Leaves of chard are an excellent spinach substitute, and unlike spinach chard tolerates summer heat. The mid-ribs can be cut into chunks and braised like celery, with melted butter and breadcrumbs to enhance their flavor. The nutritious leaves can be harvested within sixty days of sowing seed, earlier if transplants are set into the garden. Plants are hardy, can be set out several weeks before the last expected frost date, and if just a few outer leaves are harvested at a time from several plants, chard will remain productive all summer and well into winter. The two main types have white ribs or red ribs, the red creating an ornamental effect. Seeds need sowing ½ inch (1 centimeter) deep, and transplants should be spaced at least 18 inches (45 centimeters) apart in double lines along raised rows. Seed takes six weeks to reach transplant stage.* **Recommended variety:** *Ruby (red ribs).* **One-minute planting tip:** *Buy ready-grown transplants.*

## CUCUMBERS
### Warm Season

*Basically, the choice is between the slicing kinds good for using in salads and the pickle types for canning and preserves. Cucumbers like hot, sunny days, but regular amounts of moisture. They love to be planted through black plastic, which warms the soil. Although seeds can be sown directly into the planting row and covered with ½ inch (1 centimeter) of soil, earlier yields will result from transplants set 18 inches (45 centimeters) apart in double lines along raised rows. Seed takes four weeks to produce transplants. Most cucumbers have two kinds of flowers on the same plant—males and females. Only the females can set fruit, after pollination from a male, unless the variety is described as "self fertile," in which case its mostly female flowers will set fruit automatically. The most important part of growing cucumbers is to choose varieties with "triple disease resistance," otherwise you are likely to lose your plants before harvesting a crop. Also, it's important to begin spraying with a pesticide early to stop disease-carrying cucumber beetles from attacking the vines.* **Recommended variety:** *Market-more (triple disease resistant).* **One-minute planting tip:** *Buy ready-grown transplants.*

## ONIONS
### Cool Season

*There are two ways to grow onions quickly—from sets (small onion bulbs) or from seedlings (six- to eight-week-old transplants grown from seed). One-minute gardeners will do best using transplants. To start your own transplants sow seed thinly ¼ inch (½ centimeter) deep into a seed tray. It takes six weeks for seed to produce transplants. Sets are already a year old when you receive them and will put most of their energy into growing a seed stalk. The bulbs will never be as big as those that can be grown from seedling transplants. Plant sets or seedlings into the garden several weeks before the last expected frost date, since they are both hardy. Space plants 6 inches (15 centimeters) apart in double lines along raised rows. At first, onions produce "scallions," then as days get longer the base swells up into a bulb. There are many kinds of onions: yellow-skinned, red-skinned, and white-skinned; mild-flavored and hot; small, medium, and large-sized.* **Recommended variety:** *Giant Walla Walla (a mammoth, mild-flavored, yellow-skinned onion).* **One-minute planting tip:** *Buy ready-grown transplants.*

## EGGPLANT
### Warm Season

*These warm-season plants are productive only if sprayed against insect pests, particularly the flea beetle. An eggplant suffering from flea beetle damage looks as if its leaves have been hit with a shotgun blast—large areas peppered with small round holes. Transplants are best set out after all danger of frost is past and spaced 2 feet (60 centimeters) apart in a single line along raised rows. Seeds should be planted ¼ inch (½ centimeter) deep. It takes six to eight weeks to grow transplants from seed. The plants thrive under black plastic, which warms the soil early. The large, purple-black fruits start to appear within sixty days of transplanting.* **Recommended variety:** *Dusky Hybrid (heavy yielding).* **One-minute planting tip:** *Buy ready-grown transplants.*

## LETTUCE
### Cool Season

*For one-minute gardening, lettuce is best transplanted into the garden, since thinning is tedious when sowing seeds. To start your own transplants sow seed ¹/₁₆ inch (¹/₁₅ centimeter) deep. Basically there are two kinds of lettuce—*leaf lettuce, *which forms a loose rosette of succulent green leaves, and* head lettuce, *which forms tight heads. Leaf lettuce grows quickly and can be harvested just forty days from transplanting. Head lettuce takes about sixty days. Space head lettuce 12 inches (30 centimeters) apart in double lines along raised rows. Space leaf lettuce 6 inches (15 centimeters) apart. Plants are hardy and should be set out several weeks before the last expected frost date.* **Recommended varieties:** *Green Ice (loose-leaf); Buttercrunch (head lettuce).* **One-minute planting tip:** *Buy ready-grown transplants.*

## PEAS, ENGLISH
### Cool Season

*Peas used to be considered a poor crop, requiring too much space for the amount of yield. However, the introduction of Sugar Snap peas has changed all that. In addition to growing fat pods full of plump peas, the pods are edible like sugar-pod peas. They are so sweet and crunchy that they can be eaten fresh off the plant, no cooking needed. Two kinds are available: bush and vine types. Peas are best sown directly into the garden several weeks before the last frost, since they are hardy. Group several seeds together and cover with 1 inch (2½ centimeters) of soil, spacing each group 6 inches (15 centimeters) apart in double lines along raised rows. They need cool weather and regular amounts of moisture to grow quickly and produce a crop before hot weather sets in. After the vines die down by midsummer they can be removed from the row and the space devoted to a succession crop.* **Recommended variety:** *Sugar Bush (a dwarf variety requiring no support). The original Sugar Snap needs a 6 foot (2 meter) high trellis for support and is two weeks later maturing than the dwarf kinds, but it gives heavy yields, and the extra trouble of putting up supports is usually worthwhile.* **One-minute planting tip:** *Soak peas in lukewarm water for one hour, and plant those that show viability by swelling up.*

## PEPPERS
### Warm Season

*The sweet bell pepper and the hot chili pepper are popular home garden vegetables that like warm, sunny days. Bell peppers are good for eating raw, to slice in salads and use for stuffing with hamburger meat and spices. They start off green and turn either red, yellow, or purple depending on variety. Transplants are best set into the garden after all danger of frost is past, with yields beginning in seventy days. The use of black plastic as a mulch speeds maturity since peppers like warm soil. They take about eight weeks to reach transplant-size from starting seed indoors. Cover seed with ¼ inch (½ centimeter) of soil. Space plants 2 feet (60 centimeters) apart in a single line along raised rows.* **Recommended varieties:** *Big Bertha hybrid (large fruits up to 10 inches (25 centimeters) long; Golden Bell hybrid (yellow fruited).* **One-minute planting tip:** *Buy ready-grown transplants. Increase watering at time of fruit formation to avoid blossom-end rot disease.*

## POTATO, IRISH
### Warm Season

*Potatoes are best planted from small tubers set flush with the soil surface, spaced 12 inches (30 centimeters) apart in double lines along raised beds. The plants are tender to frost, and planting should be delayed until after the last frost date in spring. Growth is rapid during warm weather, and baby potatoes, or "new" potatoes, can be harvested by midsummer. The use of black plastic encourages early maturity and high yields.* **Recommended varieties:** *Katahdin (white skinned); Red Pontiac (red skinned).* **One-minute planting tip:** *Sprouted supermarket potatoes can be used as seed potatoes. Cut tubers into pieces with a green sprout on each piece.*

## PUMPKIN
## Warm Season

*Though most pumpkins are too rambling for a small garden, there are new short-vine types that can be considered space saving. Pumpkins like warm, sunny days and lots of moisture at all stages of development. Male flowers appear first, followed by fruit-bearing females. Though seed can be sown directly into the garden, after all danger of frost is past, and covered with 1 inch (2½ centimeters) of soil, earlier yields are possible by setting out transplants. Space transplants 3 feet (1 meter) apart (for short vine types) in a single line along raised rows. Seed takes four weeks to produce transplants.* **Recommended variety:** *Cinderella (a short-vine type).* **One-minute planting tip:** *Buy ready-grown transplants.*

## RADISH
## Cool Season

*The earliest varieties of radish mature in just twenty-five days from sowing seed. Cover seed with ¼ inch (½ centimeter) of soil several weeks before the last expected frost date. It is too tedious to try to grow radishes through black plastic. Radishes like cool weather and regular amounts of moisture. They are easy to grow from seed but generally need rigorous thinning to avoid overcrowding. They are not ideal for one-minute gardens but worth consideration because they are a fast crop.* **Recommended variety:** *Cherry Belle.* **One-minute planting tip:** *Pregerminate seeds indoors in a moist paper towel.*

## SPINACH
## Cool Season

*Because of its hardiness and fast growth, spinach can be planted early in the season. Once the crop is harvested, a succession crop of warm-weather vegetables can be planted in its place. Spinach can be sown directly into the garden, several weeks before the last expected frost date, covering the seed with ¼ inch (½ centimeter) of soil. Spinach is also easily transplanted. With transplants, space plants 6 inches (15 centimeters) apart in double lines along raised rows. Hybrid varieties will be ready to harvest in forty days. Spinach planted to mature as a fall crop will remain productive until Christmas. Because true spinach is so susceptible to heat, seed suppliers now offer some heat-resistant spinach substitutes, including New Zealand spinach and Malabar spinach. Both varieties remain productive all season.* **Recommended variety:** *Melody hybrid (for disease resistance and early maturity).* **One-minute planting tip:** *Pregerminate seeds indoors in a moist paper towel. Sow germinated seeds into the furrow at required spacing.*

## SQUASH, SUMMER
### Warm Season

*Though there are many kinds of summer squash, such as crooknecks and vegetable spaghetti, the most popular is zucchini squash. Hybrid varieties will start to bear within fifty days from seed. Though zucchini squash seed can be sown directly into the garden after all danger of frost is past, covering the seed with 1 inch (2½ centimeters) of soil, a faster crop is possible from setting out transplants, spaced 3 feet (1 meter) apart in a single line along raised rows. The long, slender, glossy green fruits form only on female flowers, which can be distinguished from the males by the presence of a small, immature baby zucchini already formed under the flower. To encourage an early set of fruit you can hand pollinate your female flowers by rubbing the center with a male blossom, ensuring that the powdery, yellow male pollen sticks to the female. The more you pick a zucchini squash, the more the plant is stimulated to produce more fruits. As soon as you allow a fruit to swell up large and set seeds, it will exhaust the plant of energy. Black plastic encourages summer squash to grow fast by warming the soil.* **Recommended varieties:** *Richgreen hybrid (all-female with green fruit that sets enough male flowers to ensure pollination); Goldrush hybrid (all-female with yellow fruit).* **One-minute planting tip:** *Buy ready-grown transplants.*

## SQUASH, WINTER
### Warm Season

*Most winter squashes are vigorous, vining types that take up too much room in a space-efficient garden. However, some have been bred into short-vine types, and it is these that should be selected for a one-minute vegetable garden, particularly the bush varieties of acorn and butternut squash. Winter squash generally differ from summer squash in that they mature later and keep better once picked. Winter squash form hard shells, have a fleshy interior similar to sweet potatoes in texture, and can take up to one-hundred days from seed to harvest. Though seed may be sown directly into the soil after all danger of frost is past, then covered with 1 inch (2½ centimeters) of soil, earlier harvests are assured from transplanting. Set plants 3 feet (1 meter) apart in a single line along raised rows.* **Recommended varieties:** *Jersey Golden (bush acorn type); Butterbush (short vine butternut type).* **One-minute planting tip:** *Few garden centers sell transplants of winter squash. Since it only takes four weeks to grow a transplant from seed, consider growing some of your own indoors.*

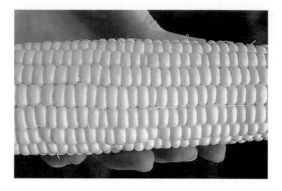

## SWEET CORN
### Warm Season

*Planting corn is easy—just sow several seeds into the soil 1 inch (2½ centimeters) deep. Space plants 12 inches (30 centimeters) apart in a single line along raised rows. Black plastic benefits sweet corn since it warms the soil. You have a choice between yellow, white, and bicolored varieties and between early, midseason, and late. Sweet corn needs regular amounts of moisture, especially when it is "tasseling." If corn is deprived of moisture at this stage, yields will be greatly reduced. Pollen from the tassels (the flower plumes on top of the plant) must fall onto the silk (the silvery threads that emerge at leaf joints). When pollination takes place an ear of corn develops under the silk and is ready for harvest when the silk has turned brown and brittle. Perhaps the biggest potential danger to a sweet corn crop is racoons. They will raid a garden when the corn is ripe and strip away every ear. Setting a portable radio in the garden at harvesttime will deter them. Some varieties of corn, called Extra Sweets, retain their sweet flavor for a long period after picking. However, in order for them to attain their super sweetness they should not be cross-pollinated with other corns.* **Recommended varieties:** *Summer Sweet hybrid (yellow); How Sweet It Is (white).* **One-minute planting tip:** *Soak seeds for one hour in lukewarm water, and plant only those that swell up.*

## TOMATOES
### Warm Season

*In addition to bush (determinate) and vining (indeterminate) kinds, tomatoes come in a wide assortment of sizes from small-fruited "cherry" tomatoes to giant-fruited "beefsteaks." Their color can vary from red and pink to orange, yellow, and white, but everyone, it seems, wants to grow large-fruited, round, red tomatoes. The kind you stake will produce fruit over a longer period than bush kinds. Tomatoes are best transplanted outdoors after all danger of frost is past, setting plants 3 feet (1 meter) apart in a single line along raised rows. Some early varieties will begin ripening fruit within fifty days. Seed started indoors generally takes eight weeks to produce a transplant. Sow seed ¼ inch (½ centimeter) deep. For one-minute vegetable gardens, tomatoes are best staked using wire cylinders called "tomato towers." The tomato plant grows up the center of the cylinder, pushes its side branches through the wire gaps, and becomes self-supporting. Then there is no need for any time-consuming tying or pruning of branches.* **Recommended varieties:** *Pixie hybrid (earliest); Supersonic (large-fruited); Supersteak (mammoth fruit, meaty, delicious).* **One-minute planting tip**: *Buy ready-grown transplants.*

## TURNIPS
### Cool Season

*New hybrid varieties of white turnips developed in Japan mature rapidly and have a sweet, moist flavor. Turnips like cool weather and lots of moisture. They are hardy and can be planted several weeks before the last expected frost date. Seed can be sown directly into the garden ¼ inch (½ centimeter) deep, a cluster of seeds to each planting station, spaced 3 inches (8 centimeters) apart. Since it is tedious growing turnips through black plastic because of the close spacing, the seed can be sown along wide, raised rows, three or four lines to a row, then covered with an organic mulch like straw. The new hybrids can be harvested as they reach the size of a golf ball, starting in just forty days. The tops are edible as "greens."* **Recommended variety:** *Tokyo Cross hybrid (white rooted).* **One-minute planting tip**: *Buy ready-grown transplants or pregerminate seeds in a moist paper towel.*

## WATERMELON
### Warm Season

*Most watermelons occupy too much space for a space-saving, labor-saving vegetable garden, but a few short-vine or "bush" types can be considered. A fertile soil, lots of sunshine, and regular amounts of moisture at all stages of development are essential for firm, flavorful fruits. Seeds can be sown directly into planting stations spaced 3 feet (1 meter) apart in a single line along raised rows. To produce the earliest yields, set out transplants after the last expected frost date. Seed takes four weeks to produce a transplant. Growing watermelons through black plastic is highly beneficial since it provides the warm soil temperature they like and promotes extra earliness. To tell when a watermelon is ripe check the tendril closest to the fruit and see if it is shriveled. Also, it's possible to judge ripeness by rapping the fruit sharply with a knuckle. If it makes a dull sound it's under-ripe; a hollow sound tells you it's ripe; a soft sound is a sign of being overripe.* **Recommended varieties:** *Yellow Baby Hybrid (yellow flesh, few seeds); Sugar Baby (red flesh, bush type).* **One-minute planting tip**: *Buy ready-grown transplants.*

**PART 2**

# THE
# ONE-MINUTE
# FLOWER
# GARDEN

# C H A P T E R 4

■

## PREPARING
## TO PLANT

■

## *Drawing Up A Plan*

CREATING A ONE-MINUTE FLOWER GARDEN IS NOT MUCH DIFFERENT FROM PLANTing a one-minute vegetable garden. With flowers, however, there is a desire to be more flexible with layouts for beds and borders. Except in the case of a flower garden strictly for "cutting," flowers are not planted in straight lines, but are best displayed in groups, sometimes in a freeform bed and other times in a mixed border. With selection of varieties for a one-minute flower garden the emphasis must be on flowers that are everblooming—or at least those that provide a long-lasting display of color from spring until fall frosts. That means a heavy emphasis on annuals and less dependency on perennials.

Except in the case of a cutting garden where flowers can be grown like rows of vegetables, the use of black plastic can present a cosmetic problem, and therefore it is necessary either to use a different kind of mulch for weed control (one that is attractive), or else cover the plastic with a decorative organic mulch, such as peat or wood chips.

Flowering annuals are much easier to grow than vegetables. Also, flowering annuals are much less work than perennials or flowering bulbs. First, flowering annuals are less susceptible to insects and disease than vegetables, many kinds tolerate long periods of drought more successfully than vegetables, and a large number of flowering annuals will thrive in shade where vegetables could never grow. Flowering annuals don't need such a fertile soil as vegetables or perennials, and the selection of ready-grown plants from garden centers is considerably greater than vegetable varieties or perennials.

Gardening with annuals is less dependent on precise timing than vegetable gardening. Many annuals will bloom within six weeks from seed and flower nonstop for ten weeks and more. Bedding plants of popular annuals can even provide "instant" color at very moderate cost. In comparison, perennials are a lot more work for short-lived color. It's a myth that perennials are easier to grow because they come up every year. The color from most perennials lasts two or three weeks, and they *still* need

*In acid soil areas, a soil test will tell you if lime should be added to the soil to adjust the pH. In alkaline soils, a soil test may indicate if sulphur needs to be used as a soil amendment and peat moss as a soil conditioner.*

## Long-Border Layout for a Flower Garden

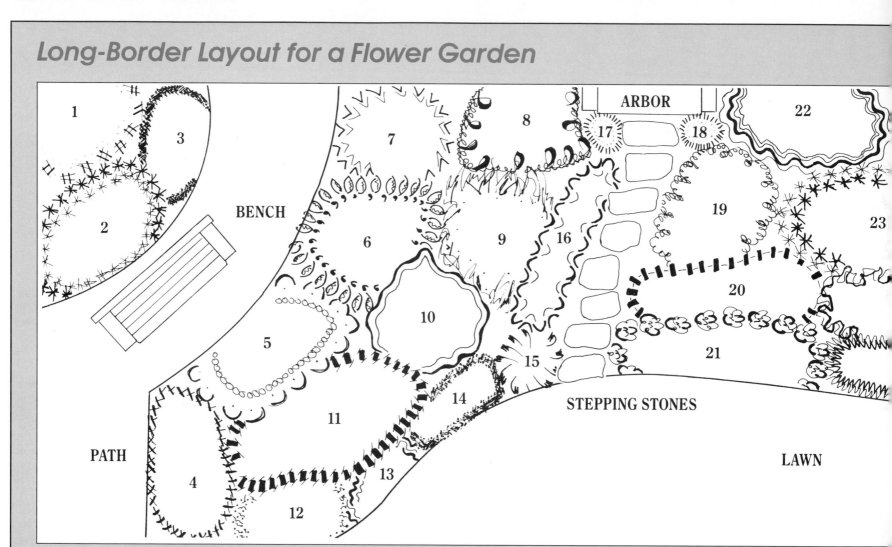

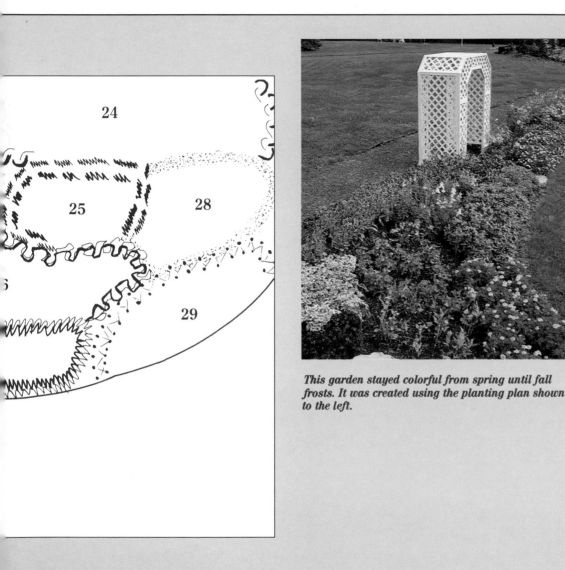

*This garden stayed colorful from spring until fall frosts. It was created using the planting plan shown to the left.*

*All the varieties featured in this display garden are not only "everblooming," remaining colorful all summer until fall frost, but they are also readily available at garden centers as bedding plants. If the exact varieties listed are unavailable, substitutions can be found quite easily in spring. Varieties with asterisks are suitable for cutting.*

   1. Geranium, Sprinter Red
*  2. Marigold, First Lady
   3. Scarlet Sage, Hot Jazz
*  4. Calendula, Gypsy Festival
*  5. Zinnias, Giant Ruffled
   6. Wax Begonias, Cocktail
*  7. Cosmos, Sensation
   8. Nicotiana Nicki Red
*  9. Snapdragon, Bright Butterflies
*10. Coleus, Wizard
*11. Celosia, Forest Fire Improved
*12. Dusty Miller
*13. French Marigold, Queen Sophia
*14. Zinnia, Small World Cherry
*15. Ageratum Blue Mink
 16. Wax Begonias, Cocktail
 17. Morning Glory, Heavenly Blue
 18. Morning Glory, Heavenly Blue
 19. Impatiens, Blitz Hybrid
 20. Scarlet Sage, Hot Jazz
*21. French Marigold, Queen Sophia
*22. Cosmos, Sensation
*23. Blue Salvia, Victoria
*24. Cleome, Rose Queen
*25. Calendula, Gypsy Festival
*26. Zinnia, Small World Cherry
 27. Petunias, Multiflora Plum Joy
*28. Dahlia, Rigoletto
*29. Ageratum Blue Mink

# Free-Form Layout for a Flower Garden

Many of the plants featured in this special display garden are not readily available from garden centers as transplants (bedding plants). However, they are quite easily grown from seed and create a special old-fashioned "romantic" appearance. Though most provide "perpetual" color from everblooming floral displays or colorful foliage, some may come in and out of bloom as the weather changes from cool to hot and back to cool again.

1. Ageratum, Blue Surf
2. Dianthus, Snowfire
3. Alyssum, Wonderland
4. Geranium Showgirl
5. Foxglove, Foxy
6. Portulaca, Sunglo
7. Nicotiana Nicki Lime Green
8. Cornflower, Blue Gem
9. Gazania Carnival
10. Dahlberg Daisy
11. Quaking Grass
12. Dusty Miller, Stardust
13. Gloriosa Daisy, Double Gold
14. Ornamental Pepper, Holiday Time
15. Scarlet Sage, Red Blazer
16. Cleome, Rose Queen
17. Coleus, Wizard Rose
18. Begonia, Vodka
19. Hardy Hibiscus, Southern Belle
20. Amaranthus, Illumination
21. Zinnia, Pinwheel
22. French Marigold Cinnabar
23. Gypsophila Covent Garden
24. African Marigold, Gold Lady
25. Blue Salvia, Victoria
26. Strawflower, Bright Bikinis

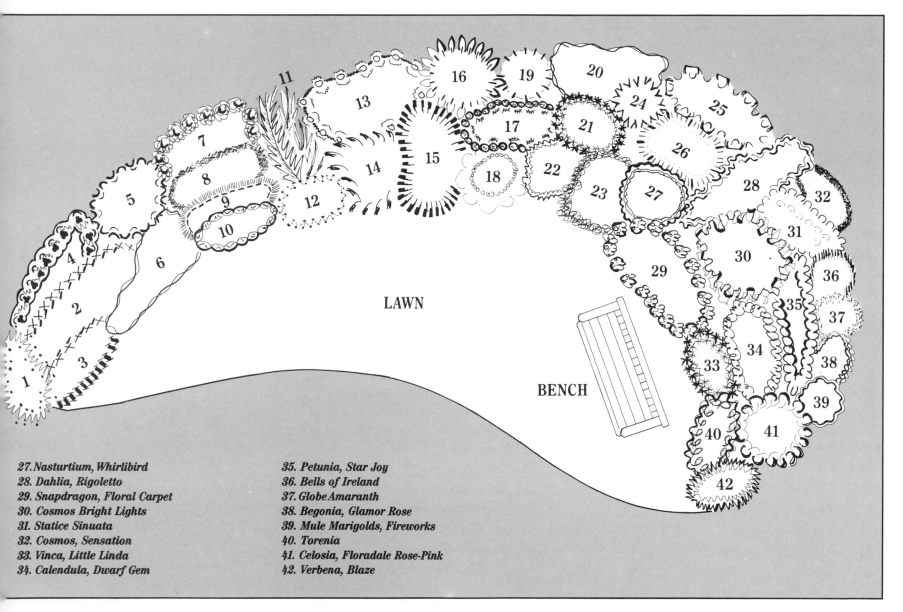

LAWN

BENCH

27. *Nasturtium, Whirlibird*
28. *Dahlia, Rigoletto*
29. *Snapdragon, Floral Carpet*
30. *Cosmos Bright Lights*
31. *Statice Sinuata*
32. *Cosmos, Sensation*
33. *Vinca, Little Linda*
34. *Calendula, Dwarf Gem*

35. *Petunia, Star Joy*
36. *Bells of Ireland*
37. *Globe Amaranth*
38. *Begonia, Glamor Rose*
39. *Mule Marigolds, Fireworks*
40. *Torenia*
41. *Celosia, Floradale Rose-Pink*
42. *Verbena, Blaze*

watering, weeding, feeding, dividing, spraying, winter protection, and usually staking to keep up their appearances. Beds of annuals, however, can be grown under black plastic to eliminate weeds, with an organic mulch over the plastic for decorative appeal and drip irrigation underneath to introduce moisture and fertilizer by the timely twist of a faucet, just as you would in a one-minute vegetable garden.

## Preparing The Soil

ANNUALS ARE MUCH LESS FUSSY ABOUT SOIL CHEMISTRY THAN ARE VEGETABLES, provided that the soil drains well and is light enough to allow roots to penetrate freely. For heavy soils, consider adding peat moss or compost.

Generally speaking, soil for flower gardens should be sandy, with plenty of organic matter mixed in to improve water-holding capacity. Most cultivated flowers (especially annuals) originate from sandy areas of the world—particularly coastal meadows and desert regions, where soils can be extremely alkaline and impoverished. Since flowering annuals are much more adaptable at growing in a wide pH range, soil tests are not so critical as with vegetables. However, if you feel a soil test is needed, follow the same procedure outlined on page 14. Obtain a soil test kit from your local county agent's office, specify that the purpose is for growing flowers, and mail the sample according to instructions (usually to a state university soil test laboratory).

Actually, for many flowering plants it is the temperature of the *soil* rather than the temperature of the *atmosphere* that determines their ability to succeed in a particular location. Even plants noted for shade tolerance, such as begonias, impatiens, and coleus, can tolerate high summer heat and full sun if their roots are kept cool. A cool soil can be provided by: adding plenty of organic material to the soil (such as peat moss, garden compost, and leaf mold); frequent watering, preferably through the use of drip irrigation; edging a bed or border with brick, flagstone or gravel; and by covering the soil with an organic mulch such as wood chips, pine needles or shredded pine bark.

Even flowers that demand full sun—such as marigolds, zinnias, and petunias—will benefit from the foregoing soil conditions. While vegetables demand plenty of sunlight, many flowers tolerate shade. An extremely colorful shade planting can be created from combining wax begonias, coleus, and impatiens, for example.

It is important to realize, however, that there are many different kinds of shade—high shade with good air circulation; low shade with poor air circulation, light shade, deep shade, morning, noon, and afternoon shade, for example. Deep shade and low shade are difficult places for plants to grow. However, the judicious removal of tree branches—particularly low branches—can often improve these difficult shade conditions enough for shade-tolerant annuals to grow.

Sunny sites can present difficulties for flowering plants if the site is too exposed to wind or salt spray or if it is a sun trap, baking the soil. An exposed location can be improved by erecting a fence or walls or by planting a hedge to cushion the force of prevailing winds. Sun traps are often caused by the slope of the ground or by light or colored surfaces such as concrete paving, stucco walls, and white-painted house siding. Frequently, the force of the sun can be weakened by planting evergreens to block the reflected heat and glare, by surrounding the planting area with grass, or by creating cool soil conditions as described in the foregoing section.

The widest range of plants can be grown on sites that have good drainage. The discussion of remedies for waterlogged sites on page 13 for vegetables applies equally to flowers. Some flowers do quite well in moist soils, and these are listed on page 79. However, there is a big difference between moist soil and waterlogged soil. A site where water remains briefly on the surface after rainfall is a quite different growing condition than a soil that remains moist from a low water table. Few flowering plants can survive in soils that puddle, and the best remedy for this, if the site cannot be drained, is to build up a foundation of crushed stones, with good topsoil placed on top, held in place with landscape ties, brick or fieldstone.

## DIGGING THE SITE

Flower beds and borders need a loose, friable soil to a depth of 12 inches (30 centimeters). Where new beds and borders need digging, any turf should be removed along with obstructions such as stones and weed roots. Where square or rectangular shapes are wanted the shape can be marked out with string. With free-form beds it is better to use a garden hose, curving it to make circles, arcs and other free flowing lines.

Use a sharp lawn edger or spade to define the edges of beds and borders. Fluff up compacted soil by digging it up and breaking it into fine particles with a rake. Soil amendments such as sand, peat moss, lime, and fertilizer can be added at this stage of ground-breaking. A well-prepared bed or border will result in a raised soil surface from the air spaces produced by digging and raking.

With island beds the soil can be mounded not only to help display plants to good effect, but also to facilitate drainage. With borders butted against a wall, hedge, or fence, the soil can be made higher at the back to make a good display surface that will also drain well.

## NO-DIG BEDS AND BORDERS

At the Good Gardening Association near London, England, there are flower beds and borders that have not been dug in more than twenty-five years. The soil is kept friable and weed-free by an application of compost in spring before plants are set into their flowering positions and again in autumn after plants have been killed by frost and their debris removed to the compost pile. The garden compost used to keep the beds loose and crumbly is made in bins using garden and kitchen waste, applied in layers. Every 6 inches (15 centimeters) of garden and kitchen waste is topped with a layer of high-nitrogen material, such as fresh animal manure or fish emulsion. The heat and decomposition produced by soil bacteria kills weed seeds so that the compost applied as a "top dressing" to the beds is weed free. Any weeds that do appear as a result of seed blown onto the compost by wind are easily removed in seconds by hand. These same techniques can be applied to beds and borders around the home.

## PREPARING TO PLANT

*Left: Flower border planted with pink spider plants, blue salvia, yellow marigolds, mauve ageratum, and purple petunias. Note the decorative mulch of shredded pine bark, which is used to deter weeds. Follow the drip irrigation long border layout for one-minute watering. Below: A detail of a one-minute flower garden demonstrates the multitude of flowers planted for cutting. Varieties include red and golden strawflowers; white multiflora petunias; pink, red, and yellow celosia; and white shasta daisies. Each group of flowers is planted in rows. The drip irrigation layout on page 24 is employed to provide effective watering.*

*Above: This one-minute flower garden resembles a wildflower meadow. Plants featured include blue corn-flowers, yellow marigolds, and pink zinnias. Note how a mulch of pine needles has been cleared from the base of the marigolds to reveal black plastic mulch, which protects drip irrigation lines and ensures weed control. The drip irrigation layout on page 72 is used to provide one-minute watering. Right: A detail of a circular flower border planted with green and pink nicotianas, scarlet sage, pink lisianthus, and silvery dusty miller shows how plants can be combined in striking ways. Note how shredded pine bark at the base of the scarlet sage provides weed control. Follow the drip irrigation island bed layout on page 72 for one-minute watering.*

## SOIL AMENDMENTS AND FERTILIZERS

Soil amendments such as sand, peat moss, and leaf mold are much more important for a productive flower garden than heavy applications of fertilizer. Indeed, many flowering annuals—such as marigolds and nasturtiums—may produce too much foliage growth at the expense of flowers in overly fertile soils.

Generally, the most important plant nutrient for flower displays is phosphorus, which is why bone meal (a high phosphorus fertilizer) is often recommended as a flower fertilizer. However, for large areas bone meal has become prohibitively expensive, and a more economical alternative for fertilizing flower beds is super-phosphate. This should be applied to the soil after it has been dug, but prior to raking level so that the nutrient particles are worked into the upper soil surface.

# CHAPTER 5

## LAYOUT AND AFTERCARE

## Creating Beds And Borders

THE BIGGEST DIFFERENCE BETWEEN A FLOWER GARDEN AND A VEGETABLE GARDEN is in the design. Whereas vegetables look attractive planted in rows and lend themselves to easier harvesting this way, beds and borders for flowers need to be different shapes and must accommodate plants in groups rather than lines. Shown on pages 72–73 is a choice of good layouts for one-minute flower gardens. Since drip irrigation is important to provide adequate moisture at the twist of a water faucet, these layouts are based on using 200 feet (60 meters) of drip irrigation hose costing as low as twenty-five dollars (thirty-two Canadian dollars, fifteen pounds), including fittings, depending on the brand.

Each layout shows an effective positioning of the drip irrigation hose and alongside it a sample planting scheme for popular kinds of flowering annuals noted for carefree maintenance and long-lasting color.

The design for a flower garden is often dictated by the presence of existing structures. In small backyards, decks, patios, terraces, fences, walls, and hedges are often excellent places to make a border. An expanse of lawn may be an ideal spot to locate an island bed. When you have decided where beds and borders should be— and how large they should be in relation to their surroundings—take a piece of graph paper and, using one square of the grid to equal 1 square foot (30 square centimeters) of space, sketch in groups of plants. Make a note of the name and color of each group and the number of plants needed to fill the designated space.

To transfer your planting plan to the garden, rake the soil surface and with a sharp stick draw an outline of the space for each flower group. Not only must you take into consideration the color harmony you wish to achieve when laying out a flower garden, but also the differing planting heights from one flower variety to another.

Most flowering annuals can be divided into three heights—tall flowers good for backgrounds, intermediate or semi-dwarf plants good for the main display area, and dwarf plants suitable as edging or low beds. Often it is possible to find these distinct heights within the same flower class—for example Climax marigolds (tall), Lady

*Cedar bark mulch used around plants repels slugs and other insect pests. Also, it is highly decorative, has a pleasant fragrance, and helps shelter drip irrigation hoses.*

marigolds (semi-dwarf) and Petite marigolds (dwarf).

To help you in making a plan, choose from among the sample layouts on pages 58–61, adapting the layout to suit your particular needs. For maximum efficiency, make beds and borders self-contained units of 500 square feet (46 square meters). To figure spacing for flowers is much easier than for vegetables. With only a few exceptions, flowering annuals benefit from a spacing of 12 inches (30 centimeters). For a bold splash of color, in most cases figure on using at least twelve plants to a group.

## Irrigation

REGULAR AMOUNTS OF MOISTURE ARE NOT SO CRITICAL TO FLOWERING PLANTS AS they are to vegetables. Many flowering annuals are drought tolerant, whereas many vegetables come under stress even after several days without moisture. Also, moisture has a big effect on the flavor of many vegetables, which is not an important consideration for flowers.

The drip irrigation systems described for vegetables are suitable for irrigating flowers. However, you may prefer to dispense with them, and if a drought does occur rely on a lawn sprinkler to irrigate flower beds. It really depends where you live and the likelihood of extended periods of drought. The occasional use of a lawn sprinkler to revive flowers from an unexpected drought is not time-consuming.

If you do decide to lay down drip irrigation, soaker hoses generally will provide greatest flexibility. They can be set in straight lines to irrigate rectangular beds or snaked to cover irregular-shaped spaces. Some sample drip irrigation layouts for flower beds and borders are shown on pages 72–73.

*Far left: A long, curving border planted with yellow dwarf French marigolds in front and scarlet sage in back is easily irrigated by two long lengths of drip irrigation hose, as in the "long border" layout on page 58. Left: Here, flowering annuals are grown in straight rows, principally to supply flowers for cutting. The drip irrigation layout for this garden could be the same as that used for the vegetable garden layout on page 24. Below: This colorful planting has flowering annuals grouped in clumps of six to twelve plants. The drip irrigation layout for the free-form border would work with this garden.*

# Drip Irrigation Layouts for Flower Beds and Borders

*The layouts shown here are for various kinds of flower plantings. Each utilizes a Y valve and two sections of drip irrigation hose connected to a water source. Care should be taken at planting time to ensure that plants are set clear of the drip lines to avoid any possibility of puncturing them. In addition to the layouts shown here, a flower garden can be planted using the layout for vegetable gardens shown on page 24, which works particularly well for cutting gardens.*

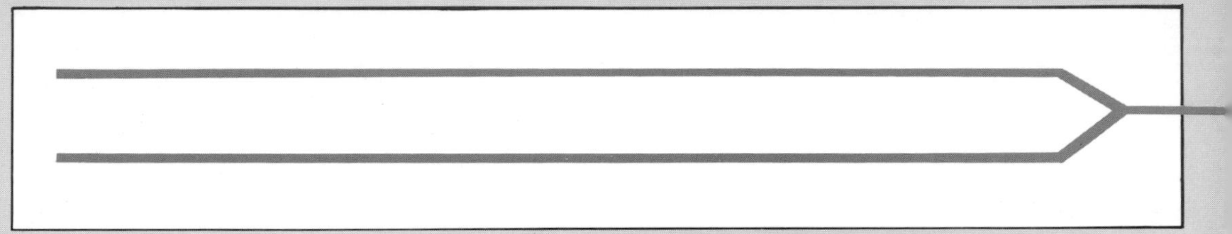

*Long Border*

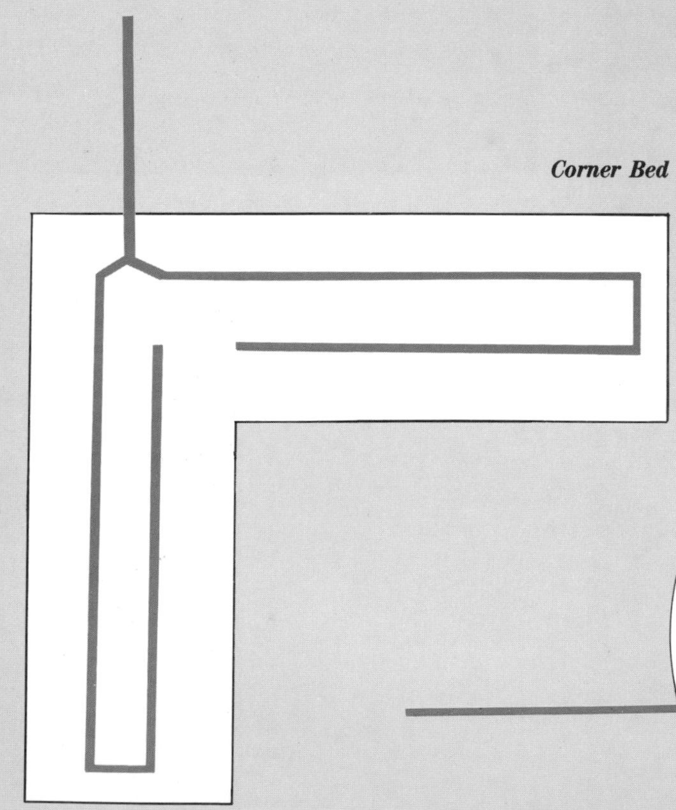

*Corner Bed*

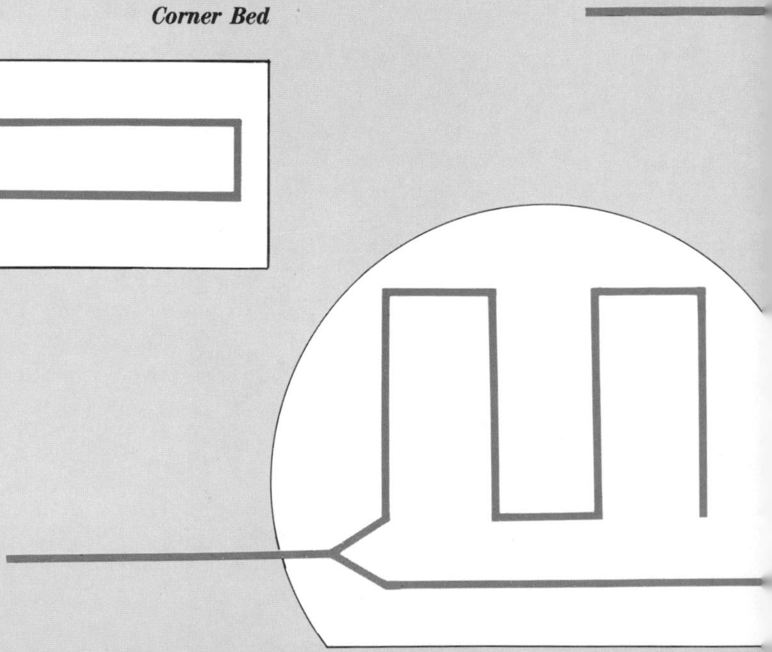

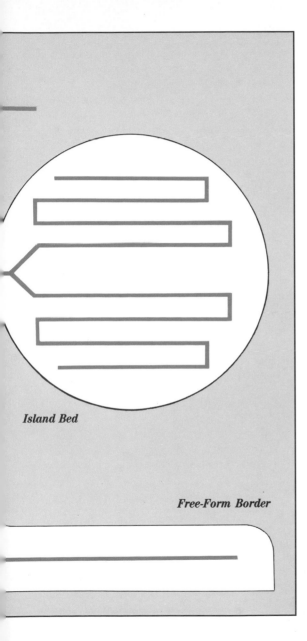

*Island Bed*

*Free-Form Border*

## Mulching

WHEREAS THE USE OF BLACK PLASTIC AS A MULCH IS RECOMMENDED FOR VEGETA-
ble gardens because of its economy and efficiency in protecting drip irrigation lines on
the soil surface, black plastic is not as aesthetically pleasing for use in flower beds and
borders. Therefore, consideration should be given to using brown fiber mulches (also
called garden or horticultural blankets) or decorative organic mulches such as wood
chips, licorice root, shredded bark, peat moss, and shredded leaves.

Organic mulches should be applied to the soil surface after soil preparation and
planting. They not only help to keep the soil temperature stabilized (on the cool side),
they conserve moisture in the soil and are an effective control against weeds.

## Pest and Disease Control

THE BIGGEST PROBLEM PESTS FOR FLOWERS ARE SLUGS. EVEN MARIGOLDS, WHICH
are repellant to most chewing insects, can be turned into skeletons overnight from
slugs, particularly after rains when dampness encourages them to venture out of
their hiding places. The most effective control against slugs is slug bait, sprinkled
where transplants have been set in the garden. Folk remedies such as setting out
pans of beer are generally ineffective since the number of slugs they actually attract
and drown are too small—less than 10 percent when tests were conducted at a major
university in a greenhouse environment.

Diseases generally are much more of a problem for flowers than insect pests.
Fungus diseases in particular, such as mildew and Botrytis disease, can cause
extensive damage and render plants brown and shrivelled. It pays to spray flowers
with a general horticultural fungicide once every two weeks during the flowering
season. Useful fungicides include Captan, Benomyl, or a general purpose fungicide
such as those sold to protect roses. The powder is very easy to apply. Generally it is
mixed with water and sprayed onto plants.

*Above: A healthy six-pack of geraniums awaits transplanting. These compact, stocky plants will put on a better display than those already in flower, pictured in the background, because plants already in flower are prone to transplant shock. Right: Plastic seed trays are used to grow flower transplants in Jiffy-7 peat pellets. When the pellets are moistened, they expand to several times their original height and make ideal pots in which to start seeds. A netting holding the peat together can be removed at transplant time to give roots freedom to grow, or seed can be started in Jiffy-9 peat pellets, which have no netting and hold the pot together with an invisible binder.*

## *Seed Starting*

THE SAME INFORMATION ON PAGE 38 COVERING SEED STARTING FOR VEGETABLES applies to flowers: the *one-step method* involving peat pellets or the *two-step method* involving starting seeds in a seed tray first and transferring to pots prior to transplanting into the garden. However, for flowers the most commonly used method of seed starting is the two-step, since most flower seeds are small and need germinating in seed trays before moving out into individual pots when the seedlings are large enough to handle. A few flower seeds—like sweet peas, nasturtiums, and morning glories—are large enough to be started in peat pellets and transplanted directly into the garden.

## Choosing Quality Transplants

FOR ONE-MINUTE GARDENING IT SAVES TIME IF YOU BUY TRANSPLANTS FROM A garden center, rather than trying to start your own from seed. Following are some tips on buying and handling transplants, also known as bedding plants:

- "Buy green." A plant that has not yet started to flower will transplant more successfully than one that is already flowering. Plants in flower are more prone to set-backs, or shock, and they bloom poorly when transplanted.

- Choose stocky, green, compact plants over plants that show yellowing or are "stretched." Stretched plants usually are under stress—from being root-bound, poorly watered, or grown in poor light.

- If plants are grown in peat pots, tear out the bottom of the pot to help release roots. Though peat decomposes in the soil, the faster the roots penetrate into the surrounding soil the better. If transplants are grown in peat pellets with netting to hold the peat in place, gently remove the netting. If you don't, roots may become confined and produce a stunted plant.

- Choose transplants that have been "hardened-off"—held in a cold frame for several days to overcome the shock of being taken from the greenhouse. Hardened-off plants will survive mild frosts, while others will be killed.

- Check stems and leaf undersides for any signs of pests, particularly small colonies of mealy bugs and aphids which can undergo population explosions when introduced to your garden.

*A well-stocked garden center is the best place to obtain plants for a one-minute flower garden. The popularity of marigolds for garden color is evidenced by the huge selection of orange, red, and yellow shades offered for sale.*

# A One-Minute Cutting Garden

*Above: A rectangular flower plot features wide, raised rows watered by a drip irrigation hose, which is covered with black plastic. Flowering annuals—a different variety in each row—are planted through the black plastic on either side of the drip line. Annual types are specially selected for cutting.*
*Right: This cutting garden comes into full bloom during summer. Because each row of plants has a 1-foot (30-centimeter) walkway separating it from the next, cutting is made easy.*

## *Maintaining Continuous Bloom*

THERE IS ONE VERY IMPORTANT JOB THAT WILL HELP TO ENSURE EVERBLOOMING plants. This is the practice of "dead-heading." Just take a few minutes over the weekend, once a week, and snap off the dead flower heads before they have a chance to properly develop seeds. This prevents seed-bearing from draining the plant of energy, and it stimulates many annuals into producing more flowers. That is why flower arrangers refer to certain plants as "cut-and-come-again."

## *Flowers for Different Needs*

**CUTTING GARDEN**
Ageratum
Bells of Ireland
Calendula
Celosia
Cleome
Cosmos
Dahlia
Marigold
Nasturtiums
Salvia, Blue
Scarlet Sage
Snapdragon
Strawflower
Vinca
Zinnia

**DRIED ARRANGEMENTS**
Bells of Ireland
Calendula
Celosia, Crested
Globe Amaranth
Strawflower

**EDGING**
Alyssum
Ageratum
Begonia, Wax
Dusty Miller
Impatiens (dwarf kinds)
Marigold, French
Pepper, Ornamental
Petunia, Multiflora
Vinca
Zinnia (dwarf kinds)

**DRY SOILS**
Dusty Miller
Globe Amaranth
Marigold
Petunia
Verbena
Zinnia

**MOIST SOILS**
Begonia, Wax
Coleus
Cleome
Hibiscus
Nasturtium
Vinca

**SHADE GARDENS**
Begonia, Wax
Coleus
Impatiens
Scarlet Sage
Torenia

# C H A P T E R 6

■

# FLOWER
## SELECTIONS

Following are types of flowers that are well suited to the one-minute flower garden. They each have an outstanding quality to contribute to the garden, whether it is nonstop bloom, attractive foliage, or versatility of display in both beds and borders. Flowering annuals are generally defined as hardy or tender. Hardy annuals tolerate mild frosts and can be transplanted to the garden several weeks before the last frost date in spring. A tender annual is usually killed by frost and should not be planted in the garden until all danger of frost has passed.

■

*The author's daughter, Tina, takes a rest from picking flowers under a white lattice arbor. This structure adds a decorative highlight to a colorful garden designed to provide nonstop blooms from spring until fall frosts.*

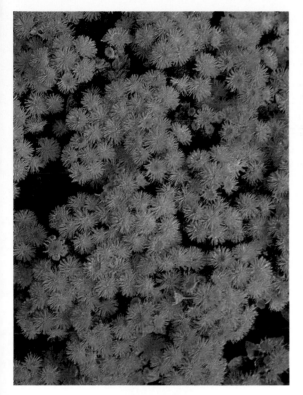

## AGERATUM
### Tender

*This annual is good for one-minute flower gardens since it blooms continuously all summer in blue, mauve, or white. Its compact appearance and 6- to 12-inch (15- to 30-centimeter) height makes it suitable for edging. Start seeds indoors six to eight weeks before the last frost date in your area. Space transplants 6 to 9 inches (15 to 23 centimeters) apart in full sun. Ageratum needs watering during dry spells to keep flowering. It also benefits from dead-heading.* **Recommended variety:** *Blue Danube hybrid.* **One-minute planting tip:** *Buy ready-grown transplants.*

## ALYSSUM
### Hardy

*Alyssum blooms continuously all summer. Growing in low mounds 3 to 6 inches (8 to 15 centimeters) high, it is suitable for edging. Colors include white, pink, and purple. Alyssum tolerates crowding, and seeds can be sown several weeks before the last frost date. Alternatively, start seeds indoors four weeks before outdoor planting to produce transplants. In the garden, space the transplants 6 inches (15 centimeters) apart. This plant needs plenty of moisture during dry spells; it flowers best in cool weather, under full sun.* **Recommended variety:** *Wonderland (award-winning rose red variety).* **One-minute planting tip:** *Blooms quickly from seeds sown directly into garden.*

## AMARANTH, GLOBE
### Tender

*These bushy annuals cover themselves in masses of clover-like flowers in white, yellow, orange, pink, and magenta. Plants grow to 2 feet (60 centimeters) high and need spacing 12 inches (30 centimeters) apart in full sun. Seeds take six weeks to produce transplants, which should be transferred to the garden after the last expected frost date in spring. Globe amaranth is good for beds and borders, also for cutting to make fresh or dried flower arrangements.* **Recommended variety:** *Buddy.* **One-minute planting tip:** *Buy ready-grown transplants.*

81

## BEGONIA, WAX
### Tender

*Begonias are topnotch annuals for one-minute flower gardens, particularly the hybrids which will bloom non-stop from the last frost of spring to the first frost of autumn and tolerate full sun better than the older standard varieties. The preferred dwarf varieties stay neat and compact, growing 6 to 8 inches (15 to 20 centimeters) high in shades of red and pink as well as pure white. Masses of these small flowers create a dramatic color impact. Foliage color can be green or bronze. Since the seeds are tiny, and seedlings require high light and constant feeding and misting to help them through their twelve-week juvenile stage, it is better to buy transplants from a garden center. Set them out in the garden only after all danger of frost has passed, spacing plants 6 to 12 inches (15 to 30 centimeters) apart. The most important requirement for spectacular flowering is cool soil. This is achieved by adding lots of peat or similar organic material, and by keeping the soil moist. Hybrids do well in sun or shade.* **Recommended variety:** *Cocktail hybrids.* **One-minute planting tip:** *Buy ready-grown transplants from a garden center.*

## BELLS OF IRELAND
### Tender

*Green flowers are rare, and bells of Ireland is the best green flower for one-minute flower gardens since it blooms from midsummer until fall frost. The plants grow two feet (60 centimeters) high and need spacing 12 inches (30 centimeters) apart in full sun. Seeds take eight weeks to produce transplants, which should be transferred to the garden after there is no danger of frost. Cutting for fresh or dried flower arrangements stimulates these plants to produce more flowers.* **One-minute planting tip:** *Soak seeds overnight to quicken germination process.*

## CALENDULA
### Hardy

*This annual blooms continuously all season, flowering profusely during cool weather on 1- to 2- foot (30- to 60-centimeter) high plants. Colors include orange, yellow, and apricot. Not only good for display in beds and borders, calendula is also excellent for cutting. Though seed can be sown directly into the garden several weeks before the last frost date in spring, transplants are readily available from garden centers. Set these 12 inches (30 centimeters) apart in full sun .* **Recommended variety:** *Gypsy Festival.* **One-minute gardening tip:** *Buy ready-grown transplants; pinch the growing tip to promote side branching.*

## CELOSIA
### Tender

*With celosia you can choose between "crested" types (cockscomb) and plumed varieties (prince's feather). Both are tender annuals blooming continuously all season in full sun. Colors include shades of red, pink, orange, and yellow. Foliage can be green or bronze. Dwarf varieties are suitable for edging and low beds while the tall varieties are excellent for cutting. For the most dramatic flower display, cockscomb should never suffer stress during its juvenile stages. If transplants are allowed to dry out, become pot-bound, or stretch toward the light, they become weaklings and never recover. Seeds take four to five weeks to produce transplants. Transfer these to the garden after all danger of frost has passed, spacing the plants 12 inches (30 centimeters) apart. Dead-heading prolongs the flower display.* **Recommended varieties:** *Fairy Fountains (plumed), Dwarf Rainbow (crested).* **One-minute planting tip:** *Buy transplants that have not yet started to bloom to avoid transplant shock.*

## CLEOME
### Tender

*This tall annual is known as spider flower for the thin, spidery seedpods that remain on the plant after the flowers fade. These plants are everblooming from early summer to fall frost, producing ball-shaped flower heads on top of ever-elongating, tall stems first flowering at 3 feet (1 meter) high and topping off at 6 feet (2 meters) high. Its colors include pink, white, and purple. The seeds need four to six weeks to produce transplants, which should be transferred to the garden after all danger of frost has passed, spaced 12 inches (30 centimeters) apart. Cleome is good for tall backgrounds and cutting.* **Recommended variety:** *Rose Queen.* **One-minute planting tip:** *Buy ready-grown transplants not yet in bloom.*

## COLEUS
### Tender

*Coleus plants are tender annuals grown more for their rainbow-colored leaves than for their flowers. In fact, to keep the plants well-groomed and long-lasting it is best to either pinch out any flower spikes that appear, or to choose a variety that has been specially bred to keep branching sideways and delay flowering until autumn. Leaf colors include red, yellow, pink, apricot, cream, and many shades of green. Leaves have many interesting shapes— some exotically ruffled. Coleus seed is tiny and takes ten weeks to produce a transplant. However, the leaf coloring shows itself immediately and remains throughout the life of the plant. Height averages 12 inches (30 centimeters); spacing should be 12 inches (30 centimeters) apart either in full sun or partial shade. Though coleus tolerate hot, dry summers they like cool soil. Plants in full sun, therefore, should receive plenty of moisture and have lots of organic matter such as peat mixed into the soil. All types are exquisite for massed bedding.* **Recommended varieties:** *Wizards.* **One-minute planting tip:** *Buy ready-grown transplants.*

## COSMOS
### Tender

*Cosmos seeds take five to six weeks to make transplants. Space them 12 inches (30 centimeters) apart in the garden. They are excellent for both garden display and cutting. Cosmos tolerate poor soils, high heat, and drought. Plant them in full sun.* **Recommended varieties:** *Sensation series (white, pink, and red daisy-like flowers);* **One-minute planting tip:** *Buy ready-grown transplants; pinch the growing tip to promote side branching.*

## DAHLIA
### Tender

*Bedding dahlias can produce a stunning nonstop floral display, provided they are watered regularly. It takes eight weeks to grow transplants from seed. Colors include red, yellow, orange, pink, and white. Most have green foliage; a few have bronze foliage. Dwarf varieties grow 2 feet (60 centimeters) high and need spacing 12 inches (30 centimeters) apart in full sun. They are excellent for bedding and cut flowers.* **Recommended variety:** *Rigoletto.* **One-minute planting tip:** *Buy ready-grown transplants not yet in bloom.*

## DUSTY MILLER
### Tender

*Several species valued for their silvery gray foliage are called dusty miller. They are best treated as tender annuals and transplanted after there is no danger of frost. The plants grow to 12 inches (30 centimeters) high and need spacing 6 to 12 inches (15- to-30 centimeters) apart in full sun. Seeds take ten weeks to reach transplant size, but garden centers always carry ready-grown plants. They are excellent as an edging around beds and borders.* **Recommended varieties:** *Silver Lace, Silver Dust.* **One-minute planting tip:** *Buy ready-grown transplants.*

## GERANIUM
### Tender

*When buying geraniums it's best to determine whether they have been grown from seeds or cuttings. Generally speaking, seed geraniums will give a longer-lasting display. If the plants are "dead-headed," flowering will continue nonstop from early summer until fall frosts. Best treated as tender annuals, geranium seeds need ten weeks to produce transplants. Dwarf varieties grow 12 inches (30 centimeters) high and need spacing 12 inches (30 centimeters) apart in full sun. Colors include red, pink, rose, and white. Some have a dark leaf zone known as a "horseshoe," considered an ornamental feature. Geraniums are excellent for mass planting in beds and borders.* **Recommended varieties:** *Ringo, Sprinter.* **One-minute planting tip:** *Buy ready-grown transplants of varieties grown from seed rather than cuttings for continuous bloom.*

## HIBISCUS, HARDY
### Tender

*The hibiscus commonly known as rose mallow that grows wild in swamps of the Southern U.S. has been hybridized to produce spectacularly large flowers up to 10 inches (25 centimeters) across, blooming nonstop from midsummer to fall frosts. Although its common name indicates hardiness, this is only with regard to the roots, which survive mild winters. Colors include white, pink, and red, some with a contrasting crimson "eye." Plants grow to 5 feet (1½ meters) high and need spacing at least 36 inches (90 centimeters) apart in full sun after all danger of frost has passed. Seeds take eight weeks to reach transplant size. Although the tops are sensitive to frost, the roots are quite hardy and if covered with a mulch after the ground freezes they will usually survive the winter to bloom again as perennials. Each flower only lasts a day, but hundreds of buds are produced in a season to ensure a continuous floral spectacle.* **Recommended variety:** *Southern Belle.* **One-minute planting tip:** *Buy ready-grown transplants not yet in bloom.*

## IMPATIENS
### Tender

*Impatiens is a top-rated annual for the one-minute flower garden, particularly in shady areas. These plants bloom from early summer to fall frost, sometimes so thick with flowers you can hardly see the foliage. Colors include red, pink, purple, white, and bicolors. Dwarf and compact varieties grow 12 inches (30 centimeters) high and need spacing 12 inches (30 centimeters) apart. Special "basal branching" varieties are especially desirable since they have a tendency to spread sideways instead of growing too tall. Seeds take ten weeks to reach transplant size, but since the seedlings are susceptible to "damping off" disease, which kills plants soon after germination (except under sterile conditions), it is best to buy ready-grown plants from a garden center.* **Recommended varieties:** *Futura series.* **One-minute planting tip:** *Buy ready-grown transplants.*

## MARIGOLD, FRENCH
### Tender

*If anything, French marigolds are even more highly rated than American marigolds for a one-minute flower garden. Although the flowers are smaller than the American types, there are more of them, and they come into bloom much earlier and last longer. Also, the color range is more extensive since it includes rusty reds and crested bicolors. The plants average 12 inches (30 centimeters) in height and can be spaced 6 to 12 inches (15 to 30 centimeters) apart in full sun. Triploid hybrids—a cross between the dwarf French and tall American marigolds—are exceptional everblooming flowers. They start to bloom within 6 weeks from seed, and since they are sterile (cannot go to seed) they put all their energy into blooming. Keep the dead blooms picked, and they will generate a density of bloom that will outshine everything else in the garden. They are exceptional for mass bedding and good for dainty cut flower arrangements.* **Recommended varieties:** *Triploid hybrids such as the Nuggets.* **One-minute planting tip:** *Buy ready-grown transplants.*

## MORNING GLORY
### Tender

*Though morning glories require support in order to climb, they are excellent flowering vines for one-minute flower gardens, growing quickly from seeds or young transplants and flowering prolifically all summer, particularly in the morning and on cloudy days.*

*The large, pea-size seeds have hard seed coats and germinate faster if soaked overnight. Varieties are available in red, pink, white, and blue, as well as some bicolors. Delay planting outdoors until all danger of frost has passed.* **Recommended variety:** *Heavenly Blue.* **One-minute planting tip:** *Soak seeds overnight in lukewarm water to quicken germination.*

## NASTURTIUM
### Hardy

*These annuals are capable of providing continuous color if they are given regular amounts of moisture, blooming best in cool weather in full sun. For a one-minute flower garden, choose the dwarf, spreading varieties. Colors include yellow, orange, red, pink, white, and mahogany. Dwarf varieties grow 12 inches (30 centimeters) high and like to be spaced 12 inches (30 centimeters) apart. The large, pea-size seeds can be sown directly into the garden several weeks before the last expected frost date. Alternatively, buy transplants or start seed indoors six weeks before outdoor planting to obtain your own transplants. Dwarf varieties are good for low beds. Long flower stems make nasturtiums suitable for cutting.* **Recommended variety:** *Whirlibird.* **One-minute planting tip:** *Plants bloom quickly from seed.*

## NICOTIANA
### Tender

*This annual has a fairly long period of bloom extending all summer. Dwarf types generally do not grow over 2 feet (60 centimeters) high and can be spaced 12 inches (30 centimeters) apart in full sun. Colors include red, pink, rose, white, and lime green. Avoid old varieties that have a tendency to close up in the afternoon. The seeds take eight weeks to produce transplants, which should be transferred to the garden after all danger of frost has passed. They are excellent for beds and borders, though unsuitable for cutting since flowers fall limp.* **Recommended varieties:** *Nicki hybrids (dwarfs).* **One-minute planting tip:** *Buy ready-grown transplants.*

## PEPPER, ORNAMENTAL
### Tender

*Although ornamental peppers tend to show color late in the season, once the yellow, orange, or red fruits start to ripen they remain decorative until fall frosts. The fruits can be round or cone-shaped on dwarf, compact plants normally 9 inches (23 centimeters) high. Plants need spacing 9 to 12 inches (23 to 30 centimeters) apart in full sun. Seed requires eight weeks to produce transplants, which should be transferred to the garden after there is no danger of frost. These are good for edging beds and for mass display in full sun.* **Recommended variety:** *Holiday Cheer.* **One-minute planting tip:** *Buy ready-grown transplants.*

## PETUNIA
### Tender

*For one-minute flower gardens the petunia multiflora hybrid varieties are better than the grandifloras. Though smaller flowered, the multifloras create a denser mass of color and are more persistent. The petals of grandifloras are easily damaged by rain and tend to exhaust themselves sooner. Plants grow to 12 inches (30 centimeters) high; colors include red, pink, rose, purple, blue, white, and bicolors. Space plants 12 inches (30 centimeters) apart in full sun. Seed takes eight weeks to produce transplants, which should be transferred to the garden after there is no danger of frost. They are excellent for mass plantings.*

*The secret to keeping petunias in bloom is to give them a "haircut" at least twice a season, as soon as plants appear to get too lanky and sparse-blooming. Do this with hedge shears to within 4 inches (10 centimeters) of the soil line.* **Recommended varieties:** *Joy series.* **One-minute planting tip:** *Buy ready-grown transplants not yet in bloom.*

## PORTULACA
### Tender

*This drought-resistant, easy-care plant is short lived compared to other flowering annuals, but it is so spectacular it deserves to be considered for a one-minute flower garden. Flowers resemble miniature roses and are produced in great abundance on succulent, spreading, low-growing stems. Colors range from white and yellow to red, pink, and purple. The purple varieties are particularly eye-catching and shimmer like satin in the sun.*

*Sunglo hybrids have especially large flowers and a good color range. Also, this variety does not close up in the afternoon like older varieties of portulaca. Plants should be planted into the garden after all danger of frost has passed. Useful for low border plantings and as edging plant in flower beds.* **Recommended variety:** *Calypso.* **One-minute planting tip:** *Flower blooms quickly from seed sown directly into garden.*

## SALVIA
### Tender

*Two kinds of salvia are suitable for one-minute flower gardens—scarlet sage and blue salvia. Scarlet sage is mostly red, though white, pink, and purple-flowered kinds are also available. Dwarf varieties grow to 12 inches (30 centimeters) high and need spacing 12 inches (30 centimeters) apart in full sun. Seeds take eight weeks to produce transplants, which should be transferred to the garden after there is no danger of frost. If the plants are watered regularly the flower spikes will continue to bloom from early summer until fall frost. Scarlet sage is excellent for massing in beds and borders.*

*Blue salvia can be treated the same as scarlet sage, but the plants tend to grow much taller. Unlike scarlet sage, which wilts when cut, blue salvia is suitable for cutting.* **Recommended variety:** *Carabiniere.* **One-minute planting tip:** *Pinch growing tip to promote side branching.*

## SNAPDRAGON
### Hardy

*Though snapdragons may stop blooming during mid-summer, they are good candidates for a one-minute flower garden since they bloom for a long time during spring, and if the spent flower stems are sheared back to within 6 inches (15 centimeters) of the soil in midsummer they will make new growth to flower nonstop from late summer to fall frosts. The semi-tall kinds are preferred since they tend to stay neat and compact, yet provide long enough flower stems for cutting. Colors include red, yellow, orange, pink and white. The plants grow 2 feet (60 centimeters) high and need spacing 12 inches (30 centimeters) apart in full sun. Seed takes eight weeks to produce transplants, which will tolerate mild frosts and can be transferred to the garden several weeks before the last expected frost date.* **Recommended varieties:** *Bright Butterflies, Coronette.* **One-minute planting tip:** *Buy ready-grown transplants; pinch growing tip to promote side branching.*

## STRAWFLOWER
### Tender

*Strawflowers are excellent for one-minute flower gardens since once they start blooming they continue all summer until fall frosts. The dwarf compact varieties not only make a dramatic display flower but have stems long enough for cutting, and they can be hung to dry to make "everlasting" flowers for dried arrangements. Colors include red, yellow, orange, pink, and white. Height depends on the variety—3 feet (90 centimeters) for dwarf types; up to 5 feet (1½ meters) for tall kinds. Space plants 12 inches (30 centimeters) apart in full sun. Seeds take six weeks to produce transplants, which should be transferred to the garden after there is no danger of frost.* **Recommended variety:** *Bikini.* **One-minute planting tip:** *Buy ready-grown transplants; pinch growing tip to promote side branching.*

## TORENIA
### Tender

*Also called wishbone flower for the intricate arrangement of stamens in the throat of each purple flower, torenia forms a neat mound of color from early summer to fall frost. These plants grow 12 inches (30 centimeters) high and need spacing at least 6 inches (15 centimeters) apart in full sun or partial shade. Seeds take ten weeks to make transplants. Torenia is excellent for edging beds and borders.* **Recommended variety:** *Mixed colors.* **One-minute planting tip:** *Buy transplants that have not yet started to bloom to avoid transplant shock.*

## VERBENA
### Tender

*This annual hugs the ground and spreads a carpet of red, white, or blue flowers that bloom for most of the summer. It grows 12 inches (30 centimeters) high. Space the plants 12 inches (30 centimeters) apart in full sun. Seeds take ten weeks to produce transplants, which should be transferred to the garden after the last expected frost date. Verbena makes an effective mass planting.* **Recommended variety:** *Sangria.* **One-minute planting tip:** *Buy ready-grown transplants.*

## ZINNIA
### Tender

*A topnotch choice for one-minute flower gardens, zinnias bloom quickly from seed and bloom a long time. Some varieties are mildew disease-resistant and bloom continuously from early summer until fall frosts. In fact, the more you pick them the more the plants are stimulated to produce flowers. Colors include red, pink, yellow, orange, and white. Plants grow 1–3 feet (30–90 centimeters) high and need spacing 12 inches (30 centimeters) apart in full sun. Though the plants will bloom within five weeks from seed sown directly into the garden, zinnias are also sold as transplants. These are excellent display flowers for mass planting and sensational for cutting.* **Recommended varieties:** *Ruffles hybrids.* **One-minute planting tip:** *Choose compact plants not yet in bloom to avoid transplant shock; pinch growing tip to promote side branching.*

## VINCA
### Tender

*This annual grows 12 inches (30 centimeters) high, blooming continuously from early summer to fall frost. Colors include white and pink with contrasting red edges. Vinca thrives on neglect and tolerates pollution. Seeds take 10 weeks to produce transplants, which should be transferred to the garden after there is no danger of frost, and spaced 12 inches (30 centimeters) apart in full sun. These plants are excellent for mass plantings and edging borders.* **Recommended variety:** *Little Linda (purple).* **One-minute planting tip:** *Buy ready-grown transplants.*

**90**

# AFTERWORD

*The one-minute-flower-gardening method not only lends beauty to the outdoors but also yields a profusion of blooms for cutting. This freshly picked arrangement demonstrates a delightful use of garden blooms.*

Whether you yearn for a bountiful vegetable garden or a colorful, everblooming flower garden, it's possible to have either or both for much less work than you would ordinarily associate with gardening. While a one-minute garden requires a little extra care in preparing the site, the aftercare is minimal, as little as a minute per day, or seven minutes on a Saturday. Most people do not mind the pleasurable part of preparing and planting a garden, nor do they mind the time required for the delightful chore of harvesting. It's the aftercare that discourages people from starting a garden or makes them give up in midseason. The work normally involved in weeding, watering, fertilizing, and fighting insect pests and disease is the hard part. But the one-minute gardener reduces all those problems to a manageable scale. Raised, wide rows improve soil depth, soil texture and soil drainage; drip irrigation supplies moisture to the root zone at the mere twist of a water faucet; black plastic (or a substitute mulch material) eliminates weeding; foliar feeding (or an automatic fertilizer applicator) supplies fertilizer effortlessly; organic pest sprays control insect pests with ease; and variety selection helps to prevent a wide range of diseases. It all adds up to the most sensible gardening system ever for anyone with little time.

What's more, neither quality nor quantity is sacrificed in the process of saving time. Vegetables yield more heavily; flowers bloom more abundantly over a longer period; even flavor and size are superior. The one-minute garden is not a gimmick, it's not an example of "poetic license," where a minute can mean more than a minute. The extraordinary fact is that the one-minute garden is truthful in every sense, and you can make it a reality inexpensively and with no previous gardening experience.

# SOURCES

## UNITED STATES

### Seeds & Supplies

Agway Inc.
Box 4933
Syracuse, NY 13221

Applewood Seed Co.
Box 10761, Edgemont Station
Golden, CO 80401

Burgess Seed & Plant Co.
905 Four Seasons Road
Bloomington, IL 61701

Comstock, Ferre & Co.
263 Main Street
Wethersfield, CT 06109

Dominion Seed House
Georgetown
Ontario, Canada L7G4A2

Henry Field Seed & Nursery Co.
407 Sycamore Street
Shenandoah, IA 51602

Gurney Seed & Nursery Co.
Yankton, SD 57079

Joseph Harris Co.
Moreton Farm
Rochester, NY 14624

H.G. Hastings Co.
Box 4274
Atlanta, GA 30302

Johnny's Selected Seeds
Box 100
Albion, ME 04910

J.W. Jung Seed Co.
Randolph, WI 53956

Earl May Seed & Nursery Co.
Shenandoah, IA 51603

McLaughlin's Seeds
Box 550 SP
Mead, WA 99021

Mellingers, Inc.
North Lima, OH 44452

Nichols Garden Nursery
1190 North Pacific Highway
Albany, OR 97321

L.L. Olds Seed Co.
2901 Packers Avenue, P.O. Box 7790
Madison, WI 53707

Piedmont Plant Farms
Box 424
Albany, GA 31703

Seedway, Inc.
Hall, NY 14463

Spring River Nurseries
Spring River Road
Hartford, MI 49057

Stokes Seeds Inc.
Box 548
Buffalo, NY 14240

Thompson & Morgan
Box 100
Farmingdale, NJ 07727

Otis S. Twilley Seed Co.
Box 65
Trevose, PA 19047

Vesey's Seeds Ltd.
York, Prince Edward Island
Canada C0A 1P0

### Drip Irrigation Systems

W. Atlee Burpee Co.
200 Park Ave.
Warminster, PA 18974

Irrigro Drip Hose
International Irrigation Systems
LPO 160
Niagara Falls, NY 14304

Smith & Hawken
25 Corte Madera
Mill Valley, CA 94941

Submatic Irrigation Systems
Box 246
Lubbock, TX 79408

Underground Moisture Control Systems
Route 4, Box 4576
Athens, TX 75751

### Pest Controls (organic)

Judd Ringer Research
6860 Flying Cloud Drive
Eden Prairie, MN 55344

Natural Gardening Research Center
Highway 48, Box 149
Sunman, IN 47041

### Soil Testing Laboratories

Except for California and Illinois, each state university offers a soil-testing service at very nominal cost. This allows you to obtain a precise analysis of your soil and recommendations for improving it. If you live in California or Illinois, check for a private soil testing laboratory in the Yellow Pages or through your County Agent.

Before sending off a soil sample, write first to the testing center for information on how to prepare and submit a sample and the cost, or check locally with your County Agricultural Agent.

Soil Testing Laboratory
Auburn University
Auburn, AL 36830

Soil Testing Laboratory
Institute of Agricultural Sciences
Palmer, AK 99645

Cooperative Extension Service
University of Arizona
Tucson, AZ 85721

Soil Testing Laboratory
University of Arkansas
Fayetteville, AR 72701

Soil Testing Laboratory
Cooperative Extension Service
Colorado State University
Fort Collins, CO 80521

Soil Testing Laboratory
Box U-102
University of Connecticut
Storrs, CT 06268

Soil Testing Laboratory
University of Delaware
Newark, DE 19711

Soil Testing Laboratory
Cooperative Extension Service
University of Maryland
College Park, MD 20742

Soil Testing Laboratory
Department of Plant & Soil Sciences
Stockbridge Hall
University of Massachusetts
Amherst, MA 01002

Soil Testing Laboratory
Michigan State University
East Lansing, MI 48823

University of Minnesota
Soil Testing Laboratory
St. Paul, MN 55101

Soil Testing Laboratory
Department of Agronomy-Soils
Drawer NY
State College, MS 39762

Soil Testing Laboratory
Agronomy Department
University of Missouri
Columbia, MO 65201

Soil Testing Laboratory
Agricultural Experiment Station
Bozeman, MT 59715

Soil Testing Laboratory
125 Keim Hall
University of Nebraska
Lincoln, NE 68503

Soil Testing Laboratory
Plant, Soil and Water Science Division
Max C. Fleischman College of Agriculture
Reno, NV 89507

College of Agricultural
Analytical Services Laboratory
University of New Hampshire
Durham, NH 03824

Soil Testing Laboratory
P.O. Box 231
Rutgers—The State University
New Brunswick, NJ 08903

Soil Testing Laboratory
Cooperative Extension Service
New Mexico State University
Box 3 AE
Las Cruces, NM 88001

North Carolina Department of Agriculture
Soil Testing Division
Raleigh, NC 27602

Soil Testing Laboratory
805 Bradfield Hall
Cornell University
Ithaca, NY 14850

Soil Testing Laboratory
Soils Department
North Dakota State University
Fargo, ND 58102

Soil Testing Laboratory
Townsend Hall
Ohio State University
1885 Neil Avenue
Columbus, OH 43210

Soil Testing Laboratory
Agronomy Department
Oklahoma State University
Stillwater, OK 74075

Soil Testing Laboratory
Cooperative Extension Service
Oregon State University
Corvallis, OR 97331

College of Agriculture
Soil & Forage Testing Laboratory
Pennsylvania State University
University Park, PA 16802

Soil Testing Laboratory
Department of Food and
    Resource Chemistry
University of Rhode Island
Kingston, RI 02881

Soil Testing Laboratory
Department of Agronomy and Soils
Clemson University
Clemson, SC 29631

Soil Testing Laboratory
Agronomy Department
Brookings, SD 57006

University of Tennessee
Soil Testing Laboratory
P.O. Box 11019
Knoxville, TN 37901

Soil Testing Laboratory
Texas A&M University
College Station, TX 77843

Soil Testing Laboratory
Department of Soils and Meteorology
Utah State University
Logan, UT 84321

Soil Testing Laboratory
Plant & Soil Science Department
University of Vermont
Hills Building
Burlington, VT 05421

Soil Testing Laboratory
Department of Agronomy
Crop and Soil Science
Virginia Polytechnic Institute
Extension Division
Blacksburg, VA 24061

Soil Testing Laboratory
Department of Agronomy
Washington State University
Pullman, WA 99163

Soil Testing Laboratory
Department of Agronomy & Genetics
West Virginia University
Morgantown, WV 26506

Soil and Plant Analysis Laboratory
University of Wisconsin
Madison, WI 53706

Soil Testing Laboratory
University Station
P.O. Box 3354
Laramie, WY 82070

# CANADA

## Soil Testing Laboratories

### Alberta

Soil Survey Unit
Canada Agriculture
Terrace Plaza Tower, 6th Floor
4445 Calgary Trail South
Edmonton, Alberta T6H 5R7

### British Columbia

Soil Survey Unit
Canada Agriculture
6660 N.W. Marine Drive
Vancouver, British Columbia V6T 1X2

### Manitoba

Soil Survey Unit
Canada Agriculture
University of Manitoba
Winnipeg, Manitoba R3T 2N2

### New Brunswick

Soil Survey Unit
Agriculture Canada
P.O. Box 20280
Fredericton, New Brunswick E3B 4Z7

### Newfoundland

Soil Survey Unit
Agriculture Canada
P.O. Box 7098
St. John's West
Newfoundland A1E 3YE

### Nova Scotia

Soil Survey Unit
Agriculture Canada
Nova Scotia Agricultural College
Truro, Nova Scotia B2N 5E3

### Ontario

Ontario Institute of Pedology
Guelph Agriculture Centre
P.O. Box 1030
Guelph, Ontario N1H 6N1

### Prince Edward Island

Soil Survey Unit
Agriculture Canada
P.O. Box 1210
Charlottetown, Prince Edward Island C1A 7M8

### Quebec

Equipe Pedologique Federale, Complex Scientifique
2700 Rue Einstein, C., 1.208
Ste-Foy, Quebec G1P 3W8

### Saskatchewan

Saskatoon Pedology Section
Saskatchewan Institute of Pedology
210 Sir John Mitchell Building
University of Saskatchewan
Saskatoon, Saskatchewan S7N OWO

### Yukon

Soil Survey Unit
Agriculture Canada
Box 2703
Whitehorse, Yukon YIA 2C6

# INDEX

Quality Printing and Binding By:
Leefung-Asco Printers Ltd
830 Lai Chi Kok Road
Kowloon, Hong Kong